PRINCIPLES & CHOICES

Book One

IDENTITY AND VALUES

by Camille Pauley and Robert J. Spitzer, S.J., Ph.D.

Nihil Obstat: Very Rev. David Mulholland, J.D.
April 12, 2012

Imprimatur: Most Reverend J. Peter Sartain
Archbishop of Seattle
Given at Seattle, Washington
on July 12, 2012.

A significant portion of the content in this text
is based on the following two books, and is used
with permission of the copyright holders:

• *Ten Universal Principles: A Brief Philosophy of
the Life Issues,* by Robert J. Spitzer, S.J., Ph.D.
(San Francisco: Ignatius Press, 2011).

• *Healing the Culture: A Commonsense Philosophy of
Happiness, Freedom, and the Life Issues,* by Robert
J. Spitzer, S.J, Ph.D. (San Francisco: Ignatius
Press, 2000).

Thank You!

The authors wish to express their profound gratitude to the following individuals and organizations who made significant contributions to this work:

Michael Pauley – Copy Editor. Major portions of Chapter 3 were written by Michael Pauley

Carron R. Silva, M.A.T. – Curriculum Design Specialist and Teaching Coach

Lynn Kittridge – Curriculum Design Specialist and Classroom Beta-Test Lead

Mark Shea – Scripture and CCC Annotations

Sheila Cowley – Graphic Design and Layout

Professional Support – Lisa-Ann Oliver, Kaelen Burton, Erika Rudzis, Monica Burrill, and Michael Friedline

Student Support – Jeffrey D'Angelo, Toni Fuller, Bayli A. Hochstein, Alyssa Kubinski, Aaron Manry, Peter Montine, Tori Moran, Maria E. Rillera, Ashlene Silva

Grateful acknowledgement is also given to the many individuals and organizations who made this work possible, including: Camille and Dale Peterson, M.J. Murdock Charitable Trust, AJ and Jody Mullally, Richard and Julie Thrasher, Holy Family Catholic Church – Kirkland, WA, John Buehler, Richard and Nancy Alvord, Robert and Annmarie Kelly, Fraser Family Foundation, Robert and Elizabeth Crnkovich, Richard and Maude Ferry, Richard and Patricia Miailovich, Alex and Stephanie Sheng, Dominic Parmantier, Bernie and Joyce Kaifer, Gellert and Elizabeth Dornay, Michelle Dotsch and Jay Hoag, Doris and James Cassan, Michael and Mary Bernard, Richard and Jill Black, John and Angela Connelly, Robert and Pam Gunderson, Stephen and Shannon Murphy, Susan Rutherford, Frederic and Martha Weiss, John and Donna Lugar, Michael and Judy Kostov.

Special thanks to the students and religion teachers at Eastside Catholic High School in Sammamish, Washington and McGill-Toolen High School in Mobile, Alabama, for serving as the beta-test sites for our pilot study.

About the Authors

Camille Pauley is the creator and principal author of the *Principles and Choices©* high school curriculum. She is also the author of the *Robert and Emma* series—a play in four acts. Camille is president and co-founder of Healing the Culture, which educates people on the unique dignity of human life; and founder of Being With, which trains individuals to provide compassionate visitation to people with debilitating or terminal illnesses or injuries. Camille has spoken to thousands of audiences, has co-produced six video series, and has been an influential voice on social media, television, radio, and print media. She holds an M.A. in Communication from Washington State University. She and her family live in Seattle, Washington.

Robert J. Spitzer, S.J., Ph.D., is the author of the books upon which the *Principles and Choices©* curriculum is based, including *Healing the Culture* and *Ten Universal Principles*. He is co-founder of Healing the Culture, and former President of Gonzaga University. Fr. Spitzer has inspired millions of people with his books, video series, television programs, and lectures on everything from the dignity of the human person to proofs for the existence of God. He holds a Ph.D. in Philosophy from Catholic University of America. Fr. Spitzer is founder and President of the Magis Institute for Faith and Reason in Garden Grove, California, through which you can purchase the popular high school curriculum: *The Reason Series: What Science Says About God*, and other resources.

Contents

Check it out!

Enter the codes you'll find in your textbook here...

www.principlesandchoices.com

Like us on Facebook and share your thoughts...

www.facebook.com/principlesandchoices

Follow our tweets for up-to-date news and views...

twitter.com/prinandchoice

Check out videos from our team and friends around the world...

www.youtube.com/user/principlesandchoices

PRINCIPLES & CHOICES

Book One

IDENTITY AND VALUES

ARE YOU HAPPY? ARE YOU REALLY, TRULY HAPPY?

THINK ABOUT THAT QUESTION FOR A MINUTE.

"Happiness is not being pained in body or troubled in mind."
— Thomas Jefferson 3rd President of the United States

"ALL YOU NEED FOR HAPPINESS IS A GOOD GUN, A GOOD HORSE, AND A GOOD WIFE."
— Daniel Boone Pioneer, Explorer, and Frontiersman

"It isn't necessary to be rich and famous to be happy. It's only necessary to be rich."
— Alan Alda Actor, Director, Screenwriter, and Author

"[Happiness] is not attained through self-gratification, but through commitment to a worthy purpose."
— Helen Keller Author, Political Activist, and Lecturer

"Being the richest man in the cemetery doesn't matter to me... Going to bed at night saying we've done something wonderful... that's what matters to me.."
— Steve Jobs Entrepreneur, Businessman, Inventor, and Co-founder of Apple Inc.

"The greatest happiness of life is the conviction that we are loved, loved for ourselves, or rather loved in spite of ourselves." **— Victor Hugo** Poet, Playwright, Novelist, Essayist

beauty

being with

common cause

crisis

desire

doing for

dominant

empathy

ego-gratification

happiness

intangible

justice

love

materialism

purpose

tangible

transcendental

truth

ultimate good

unconditional

unity

CHAPTER 1:

Happiness

Happiness gets a lot of attention. Billions of people are looking for it, trillions of dollars are spent pursuing it, and tens of thousands of books have been written about it.

If you search "what is happiness" on the Internet, you will find tens of millions of answers. There is no shortage of advice on how to find it.

When people are asked, "What makes you happy?" they often respond: "being healthy," "getting what I want," and "being liked." But is it possible to be happy without these things? And is it possible to achieve all these things and still not be happy?

For many, happiness seems so elusive. Why is that?

Socrates was a Greek philosopher who developed our modern Western system of education nearly 2,400 years ago. Among many other insights, he taught that true happiness comes from the cultivation of virtue, and that the ultimate goal of education is to learn how to rank our human desires and develop virtuous habits so that we can achieve real happiness.

This idea was novel and risky in his time. Most people believed that happiness was not something that resulted from human effort, but was arbitrarily granted by the gods to some and not to others. As a result of his teachings, Socrates was convicted of "corrupting the youth" and was forced to drink from a deadly cup of hemlock as punishment, but his teachings lived on. His student Plato passed on these ideas to his own student, Aristotle, who became one of the greatest thinkers in the history of science and philosophy.

Aristotle was the first person to introduce "happiness" as an entire field of study. He believed that all students deserve an education that goes beyond learning a skill, to actually learning how to live a "good life," which includes the development of moral character.

Unfortunately, many people do not spend much time reflecting on what happiness really means and what life is all about. As Aristotle noted, this can cause us to accept popular definitions of happiness that focus on materialism and ego-gratification, which negatively affect the way we define success, quality of life, love, suffering, freedom, good, evil, justice, and injustice. He wrote in the *Nicomachean Ethics*: "The mass of mankind are evidently quite slavish in their tastes, preferring a life suitable to beasts" (1095b 20).

**What does Aristotle mean by:
"slavish?"
What does he mean by the phrase:
"a life suitable to beasts?"**

This course was designed to help students avoid that fate by offering what Socrates and Aristotle advocated for and what many people sadly neglect: a chance to seek wisdom about happiness and meaning in life, and to investigate some of the most important moral issues that affect our pursuit of virtue and moral character.

To the very end, Socrates held fast to what he believed, and encouraged his students to pursue not just increased *knowledge*, but a love of *wisdom* grounded in *truth*.

Just as Socrates and Aristotle did, this book takes definite positions about the kinds of behaviors and attitudes that lead to deep and lasting happiness, and those that do not. Some of these positions are not popular. Some are difficult and require great personal sacrifice. But they are all worthy of examination.

At the trial before his death, Socrates said: "The unexamined life is not worth living." So we encourage you to examine your own life and the positions in this book, to ask questions, and to use your intellect and freedom to pursue goals that are worthy of you as a human being. That is what a good education is all about.

THE FOUR LEVELS OF HAPPINESS

A *desire* is an anticipation of something we do not yet have which causes an emptiness inside and a yearning to be fulfilled. Every desire seeks fulfillment. *Happiness* can be defined as *the fulfillment of a desire*. When a particular desire is fulfilled, we experience a particular kind of happiness. When a desire is unfulfilled, we experience a kind of unhappiness.

Every human being will make decisions about which desire is most important. We will make that desire *dominant*—meaning that we will give it priority in our lives—and this dominant desire will become our self-identity, or our meaning and purpose in life. For example, a person can make the desire for popularity her whole purpose in life. She will do, say, and wear things that will make her more popular. She will choose popular friends, and will avoid things that might make her less popular. Alternatively, she might decide that being a good friend is her purpose in life, in which case she will be more concerned about being kind, generous, compassionate, and helpful, than about how she looks or what other people think of her. Or she might choose graduating from school or getting to heaven as her purpose in life. Obviously, we can always change our mind about our most important desire, and that will change how we view our purpose in life.

Notice that there are different kinds of desire and different kinds of happiness. Some desires show us what we have in common with animals (like our desires to eat and to escape from danger). Other desires show us what we have in common with God (like our desires for truth, love, and justice).

Philosophers have sometimes referred to these kinds of happiness as "levels of desire" or "levels of happiness" because they can be ranked from lowest (least fulfilling) to highest (most fulfilling). Most philosophers explain that lower levels of happiness are easier to get, are *tangible* (which means that you can experience them through your five senses), require less personal sacrifice, don't last very long, and are not deeply fulfilling.

Tangible means that it can be perceived through the five senses.

On the other hand, higher levels of happiness tend to be more challenging to achieve. They are experienced through the heart rather than through the physical senses (they are intangible). They require more personal sacrifice, but they also last longer and are more deeply fulfilling.

Philosophers have identified four different levels of happiness, which will be explored in the next pages.

WE CAN ALWAYS CHANGE OUR MIND ABOUT OUR MOST IMPORTANT DESIRE, AND THAT WILL CHANGE HOW WE VIEW OUR PURPOSE IN LIFE.

Brainstorm definitions of the following words: Desire, Happiness, Purpose.
Then, use your phone, tablet, or computer to find at least three different definitions for each word. Finally, answer the following questions:
> What makes you happy?
> What makes you unhappy?
> What are the typical desires of people your age?
> What do you think people your age would typically list as their purpose in life?

LOWER LEVELS OF HAPPINESS

Easier to acquire
Tangible
Less personal sacrifice
Short term
Not deeply fulfilling

HIGHER LEVELS OF HAPPINESS

Challenging to acquire
Intangible
More personal sacrifice
Longer lasting
Deeply fulfilling

What is your purpose in life? Spend some time thinking about it, and then take a separate sheet of paper and write down what you think is the most important desire in your life. (Jot a few notes below to start if you want.) Whether or not you realized it before, this is how you define your purpose. Think about how this purpose is affecting all the decisions you make on a daily basis. Think about how it is affecting your relationships. Think about how it may be affecting your future. Write these thoughts down. If you like what you have written, then jot down some ideas about how you can achieve this goal. If you don't like what you see on the paper, you can change it. If you're not sure what you think, set the paper aside. You can come back later and review what you've written.

© auremar / Fotolia

Four Levels of Happiness

Level 1   Physical Pleasure and Possessions

Comes from an external stimulus (something outside of me), like the warm sun or a sweet ice cream. Interacts with one or more of the five senses. Offers immediate gratification. Does not require skill or training. Is concrete, direct, tangible, and often quite intense.

CRISIS 1: Does not extend beyond myself, is not long-lasting, and does not use my higher powers. Therefore, I eventually become bored and empty, and feel as though I am living beneath myself.

Level 2   Ego-Gratification

Comes from achievement, winning, power, and popularity. Requires skill and control, and seeks comparative advantage. Offers short term gratification.

CRISIS 2: Does not extend beyond myself, is not long-lasting, and uses only some of my higher powers. Leads to jealousy, fear of failure, aggression, ego-sensitivity, blame, rage, self-pity, inferiority, superiority, suspicion, bitterness, contempt, resentment.

Level 3   Good Beyond Self

Comes from doing a greater good beyond myself, and being with others in empathy. Seeks to satisfy the human desire for truth, love, justice, beauty, and unity. Extends beyond myself, offers long term gratification, and uses my higher powers.

CRISIS 3: My desire for perfect, absolute, infinite, unconditional, and eternal Truth, Love, Justice, Beauty, and Unity cannot be fulfilled by this world. Attempting to fulfill these desires only through human beings and the things of this world will lead to frustration, dashed expectations, and despair.

Level 4   Ultimate Good

Comes from receiving and participating in ultimate (perfect, absolute, infinite, unconditional, and eternal) Truth, Love, Justice, Beauty, and Unity. Can only be achieved by believing that ultimate Truth, Love, Justice, Beauty, and Unity exists as a reality (God). Extends beyond myself infinitely, is eternally enduring, and infinitely deep.

CRISIS 4: Feelings of being abandoned by God. Refusing to allow God to come to me, and trying to get to Him by myself (which is impossible, because He is infinite and I am finite). I can avoid this crisis by practicing humble surrender to God's love through prayer, and allowing Him to come to me.

Use code PCS112 to download and print copies of the Four Levels of Happiness Chart.

© Fertnig / iStockphoto

HAPPINESS 1

Happiness 1 is the kind of happiness we get from physical pleasure and possessions. It is **tangible**, which means that it involves something we can sense through touch, sight, smell, taste, or sound. So when something is physically pleasing to us, or when we possess some physical thing that we want, we experience Happiness 1.

For example, you're really stressed out about school. You come home tired and hungry, serve yourself a large slice of cake, grab a pop from the fridge, plop down on the couch, and watch TV. That would be an experience of Level 1 through several of the five senses.

Four Key Characteristics of Happiness Level 1

1] **It is immediately gratifying.** You slip into character in your favorite action-packed computer game and your senses are immediately thrilled by the adrenaline rush.

2] **It doesn't last very long.** Each rush lasts only a moment. When the game is over, the pleasure is over. If you play too much, you can get disoriented, tired, or sick.

3] **It doesn't require much from you.** Even people without any skill or experience can slip into the virtual world and feel some level of exhilaration.

4] **It doesn't positively affect anyone outside yourself.** Other people watching you play the game do not feel the same thrill that you do, and wish you would hurry up and finish so that they can have a turn.

Some people mistakenly believe that Christianity teaches that physical pleasure is evil. This does not appear to be what Christ taught. Of the 35 recorded miracles that Jesus performed, 23 of them included physical healings, so physical well-being would appear to be important to God. In fact, the very first public miracle that Jesus performed was transforming water into wine at the wedding feast in Cana. In Scripture we see that Happiness 1 is not bad in itself. It's not wrong to want to have your physical needs met, and it's not bad to enjoy physical pleasure. We are, after all, the unity of a soul AND a body — and the body has needs as well as the soul.

From a Christian perspective, it is good to enjoy physical pleasure and possessions. God gives these things as gifts in order that we might be physically healthy and whole. If human beings did not enjoy things like food, water, warmth, shelter, health, and sex, we would not seek them, and would become extinct.

"God looked at everything He made, and found it very good."

(Genesis 1:31)

But Christianity also teaches that it is harmful to pursue physical pleasure at the expense of spiritual fulfillment. Most of us have abused Level 1 and used it in ways that are not healthy. For example, we can indulge in foods that may taste good but are not good for our bodies. We can listen to music that may be stimulating but leaves us feeling angry or alienated from others. We can enjoy computer games but shut out the rest of the world and ignore our responsibilities to family, friends, and school. We can use money for selfish purposes. We can use people for sexual gratification and fail to respect the sacred dignity and purpose of human sexuality. The abuse of Level 1 can lead to what might be termed "Crisis 1."

CRISIS 1

Animal scientists have noted for centuries that an animal's highest prioritizations are always to seek food, safety, shelter, reproduction, and rest. When they experience hunger, danger, bad weather, mating season, or exhaustion, animals cannot ignore their most basic biological needs. It is what drives them. But human beings *can* choose to ignore biological desires. We can consciously *choose* what our highest priorities in life will be. We can make deliberate decisions about the meaning and purpose of our lives, and about what is most important to us.

For example, a high school student might decide that the most important thing in the world is his girlfriend. He sacrifices other things that he wants in order to save his money and buy her gifts. He sacrifices comfort by giving her his jacket when it begins to rain. Because he wants what's best for her, he chooses to sacrifice his sexual impulses and wait until marriage. He sacrifices sleep to finish writing her a love letter. He may even choose to face injury, persecution, or death in order to protect her from danger.

Alternatively, he can choose to make Happiness 1 the most important thing in life. He can choose to place material pleasures and possessions above what is good for his girlfriend and even above all other matters in life. He can seek physical things as his highest priority.

Research (and experience) shows that when human beings live for Happiness 1 as our highest priority, we eventually become **bored** with the things we used to enjoy. We experience **loneliness, emptiness,** and a

There is nothing wrong with Happiness Level 1. It's good to enjoy physical pleasure and possessions in moderation. However, we can abuse Level 1 and use it in ways that are unhealthy. List some ways that you have seen people abuse Level 1.

_____

_____

_____

_____

_____

_____

_____

_____

_____

_____

_____

_____

_____

_____

_____

lack of direction. We begin to feel like we are **living beneath ourselves.** And we develop **low self-esteem** (a sense that we are no more valuable than the things with which we are so obsessed).

In an article entitled, "In Pursuit of Affluence, at a High Price," [A] the New York Times reported on a growing number of psychological studies concerning people who make material pursuits, like money, luxury, and beauty, (what we have called "Level 1") their number one priority. These studies all found that such people experience significantly increased **anxiety, depression,** and **physical discomfort;** use more **cigarettes, alcohol, drugs, and television;** and have **lower self-esteem** and a **lower overall sense of well-being** than people who place less emphasis on material things.

Dr. Richard Ryan, professor of psychology at the University of Rochester, was quoted as saying, "The more we seek satisfactions in material goods, the less we find them there. The satisfaction has a short half-life; it's very fleeting." It was particularly interesting that these studies were consistent across all ages, levels of income, and cultures. Also, the article made the important distinction that it's living for Level 1, and not just enjoying Level 1, that causes the problem. The article concluded that "affluence (wealth), per se, does not necessarily result in an unsatisfying life. Problems are primarily associated with 'living a life where that's your focus.'"

Notice that when an animal lives only for physical comfort and then achieves physical comfort, it is content. But when a human being does the same thing, the human being is unhappy. When we read the biographies and even autobiographies of people who spent their lives obsessing on Happiness 1, we find that many of them ended up lonely, alcoholic, addicted to drugs, sexually promiscuous, depressed, suicidal, abusive, and abandoned by friends and family. A brief glance at some of the celebrity headlines in the checkout line of the grocery store will reveal this same sad story.

Take some time to consider your own personal experience. Have you ever chosen to make material pleasures and possessions more important than other goals in life? If so, do you remember how it made you feel? Did you notice any of the negative feelings and attitudes mentioned in bold in the left column? Did you notice anxiety, boredom, or low self-esteem? Did depression start creeping in? Did you begin to feel like you were living beneath yourself? Did you find yourself becoming addicted to distractions like television or computer games? Did you experience a negative overall sense of well-being? If so, you might ask yourself another question: "Is this what I think real happiness should be like?"

> ## "THE MORE WE SEEK SATISFACTIONS IN MATERIAL GOODS, THE LESS WE FIND THEM THERE."
>
> **- Dr. Richard Ryan, University of Rochester**

When they think about it, most people agree that Happiness 1 doesn't bring deep or lasting happiness. Dr. Richard Ryan's words seem to ring true: "It's very fleeting." Fortunately, there is a way out of the problems caused by Crisis 1. In fact, it can help us to avoid the crisis altogether.

As you look through the "Four Levels of Happiness" chart on page 5 you may notice that each higher level becomes more intangible than the last. This means that the higher levels get less and less physical, and so we do not need our five senses as much to enjoy them. Also, the higher we move up the chart, the more challenging each Level gets, because each level requires more personal sacrifice than the level before it. But each higher level also lasts longer and is more deeply fulfilling than the one before it. In other words, as we move up through the higher levels on the chart, our workload increases, but so does our reward. These differences will be discussed in greater detail as we go through each of the higher levels. In the meantime, the following advice may be helpful:

In order to make Happiness 1 healthy (and avoid Crisis 1), use Level 1 as a means to a greater end. Instead of making Level 1 our priority and seeking it as our ultimate goal, we can choose to take care of our physical needs for the purpose of pursuing higher levels of happiness.

Some philosophers have suggested that any time a Level 1 pursuit gets in the way of a Level 2, 3, or 4 goal, it will lead to crisis and should be avoided. They advise keeping our sights on the higher level of happiness. You can post your own helpful tips and ideas for avoiding Crisis 1 at **www.principlesandchoices.com**

HAPPINESS LEVEL 1: PHYSICAL PLEASURE & POSSESSION

CRISIS: BOREDOM, EMPTINESS, FEELINGS OF LIVING BENEATH MYSELF

Where did these Four Levels of Happiness come from?

For thousands of years people have observed that there are different kinds of happiness. Plato and Aristotle wrote about different types of happiness 2,400 years ago. So did other historical thinkers like Soren Kierkegaard, Karl Jaspers, Saint Augustine, Martin Buber, Viktor Frankl, Abraham Maslow, Thomas Aquinas, and Lawrence Kohlberg. Happiness has been studied by philosophers, psychologists, theologians, sociologists, anthropologists, historians, and others. These four levels of happiness can be found in nearly all religions, and they reach maturity with the Golden Rule and the Beatitudes, which reflect the love revealed by Jesus Christ. Throughout the last 3,500 years you can see these levels again and again in the cultures of North and South, East and West.

We have summarized thousands of years of observation and reflection from hundreds of great minds, and grouped their findings into four distinct kinds, or levels, of happiness.

As you read the next few sections, you will probably find that you have a lot of questions, like:

> Why does it stop at four? Are there more levels?

> Why is Level 4 the highest?

> Can you have all of the levels at once?

> What if I don't agree with these levels?

Use code **PCS113** to get answers to these and other "Frequently Asked Questions." There's also a place for you to ask your own questions.

HAPPINESS 2

Happiness 2 is ego-gratification. *Ego* is the Latin word for *I*. Thus, Happiness 2 comes from feeling good about yourself. It is usually experienced in one of the following four ways:

1] winning or being better than others

2] achievement or success

3] power or control

4] popularity or admiration

So, for example:

> **Angela** tries out for the cheerleading squad, and is awarded team captain for being a better cheerleader than any of the other students (winning).

> **Michael** builds a robot for science class, and it successfully climbs five steps (achievement).

> **Elijah's** parents go out for the evening and give him charge over his two younger brothers (power).

> **Vanessa** gives each of her classmates a gift card for Valentine's Day, and suddenly everyone wants to be her friend (popularity).

Each of these teenagers is experiencing a type of Level 2 happiness. Notice that Level 2 almost always involves comparing ourselves to other people, and tries to focus the attention and approval of others on ourselves.

Now, if somebody makes Level 2 dominant in his life (if he is living for Happiness 2 as his highest priority) he would constantly have to compare himself to everyone else and ask, "Who's winning? Who's losing? Who is more successful? Who is more powerful? Who's more popular?"

© DaydreamsGirl / iStockphoto

Growing up in the middle of a big family made it difficult for me to find my way. My older siblings were smarter and more musically talented than I was. My younger siblings were more athletic and made friends easier than I did. But when I reached high school, I discovered a talent for public speaking. I found that I could stand in front of an audience and I wasn't afraid. I could write an interesting speech and was really quite good at memorizing and delivering it. The audience would laugh at my jokes, listen intently as I made my points, and would clap and sometimes even stand up and cheer out loud at the end. It was my first real taste of Happiness Level 2.

Eventually, I joined the school forensics team, and became a champion public speaker and debater. My coach loved me and the other students admired me. I was feared by opposing schools, and usually came home from tournaments with more than one trophy and my name mentioned in the local paper. I was a rising star.

But then I graduated and went away to college. College was a bigger world than I had ever experienced. There were a lot of people from all over the country, and even all over the world — a lot of *very talented* people. My first college debate tournament was a complete humiliation. The rules were new and I didn't understand the topics we were given. My coach was disappointed in my performance, and my debate partner was crushed and embarrassed by how much I stumbled during the rounds. It pretty much went downhill from there. I won a few and lost a lot, and grew more and more resentful of the other team members who seemed to be doing much better than I was.

One day Tomi, a member of our team, came to the debate room late in the evening and saw me poring over debate handbooks and boxes of evidence cards. Tomi was known for sometimes placing first or second at tournaments. "What are you doing here so late?" he asked. "I want to win," I said. "Winning isn't everything, you know." I glared at him and answered, "It is to me."

Tomi shrugged, sat down, and began to teach me how to debate, *his way.* I learned how to become aggressive in debate rounds and pound into my opponents. When I didn't understand something, he showed me how to fake it, and even how to make up evidence. And then, like icing on the cake, he showed me how to "spread." That's what we called it when a debater would talk so fast in a round that no one else could keep up. The other debaters would be left stunned. Sometimes by spreading you could even fool the judges. They wouldn't be able to keep up either, but they didn't want to admit it. So they would just give you the win and write about what a great debater you were. I tried it, and it worked. Sometimes I lost. But mostly, I won.

When I graduated from college, I went to work for an advocacy organization that fought for justice among disadvantaged and vulnerable groups of people. The organization hired me because I was a good public speaker. I would travel around the country and speak to large groups of people, arguing for our cause. People would listen intently, and at the end of every speech, they would all clap and tell me what a great speaker I was. But I didn't feel very great about it. I wasn't sure that I was actually changing their minds. But they thought I was smart, and that was what mattered to me. Or so I thought.

> ## "I NEVER FORGOT THAT SINKING FEELING IN MY HEART."

One day after a particularly important speech, an older member of the audience approached me. He was a physician, and a distinguished member of the faculty at a local medical school. I had been told by the host of the event that it would be very important to convince this particular man to support our cause. The physician smiled at me and said softly, "You're a very good speaker, but...." I was caught off guard by the word "but" and so I said, "Thank you...but what?" His eyes narrowed and his smile disappeared as he said, "But you intimidated the heck out of me." And he turned around and walked away.

I never forgot that sinking feeling in my heart. It was a feeling that told me I was living beneath myself. I was pursuing something that didn't really matter, and leaving a very vulnerable group of innocent people without a true advocate — all because of my own need to look powerful and impress people. I never felt so low in all of my life. But it was a very good lesson for me, and the beginning of my journey into Happiness Level 3.

— Anne

Briefly review Anne's story, and see if you can identify how she experienced each of the four Level 2 goals (see the list on page 10). Underline or circle what you find in the story, and write down next to it which of the four goals she experienced in that part of the story. Then, use the space below to write or draw about how you have experienced each of the four Level 2 goals.

Three Key Characteristics of Happiness 2:

1] **It is short term, but lasts longer than Level 1.** Remember that in Level 1, the happiness only lasted as long as the physical rush, and then it was over. But in the story on page 11, you can see that when Anne won a debate tournament, she got an ego-high that could last until the next tournament (or until other people forgot or stopped caring about it).

2] **It requires some skill, talent, or intelligence.** Anne had some natural talent as a public speaker, but found that when she went to college, she had to work harder at it in order to succeed.

3] **It affects more people outside yourself than Level 1.** Anne's debate partner, her coach, and her team were all affected when she would win or lose a tournament. She could also affect her entire school (by bringing home several trophies), her audience (by making them laugh or applaud), and her community (which would proudly publish her name in the newspaper). Although she doesn't mention them, her family and friends also probably felt a sense of solidarity with her, and would get excited when she won, and feel her pain when she lost.

As with Level 1, Level 2 is not bad. In fact, it can be very good. The desire to be better than others can motivate us to make improvements for the human community — like when a car company designs a vehicle that gets better gas mileage than other cars on the road. The desire for success is important for the progress of civilization — like when scientists make new discoveries that help to cure diseases like cancer. The need for power and control can be very important for managing a team or directing people — like when a firefighter is trying to direct people to the nearest exit in an emergency. The desire for popularity is useful if you are trying to do something good and need the support of other people — like when a citizen wants to be elected the new mayor of a city in order to help end corruption and attract businesses that will create new jobs.

Making Level 2 a higher priority than Level 1 can help to keep Level 1 in check. For example, if a college graduate has made it his priority to get into a top-rated law school, he is probably not going to stay up all night partying with his friends right before the qualifying exam. He is going to get a good night's sleep and avoid anything that will impair his thinking skills, memory, and good judgment.

So what's the problem? The problem is not Level 2, but *living for* Level 2 as our highest priority in life. It's making Level 2 an end in itself, instead of a means to a greater end. We can abuse Level 2. Like Anne in the story on page 11, anyone can choose to live for ego-gratification as if it were the most important goal in life. But if we do that, we will be focused on being better than everyone else, being more successful, having more control and power, and being more popular and admired. Life will become a big, aggressive competition. That may be fun for a while, but eventually it may lead to Crisis 2.

Think about characters in books, movies, songs, or history who turned a Level 2 goal into the most important goal in life. What happened? Be prepared to bring some examples to share with the class.

_____

_____

_____

_____

_____

There is nothing wrong with Happiness 2. The world needs high achievers and strong leaders. But if we make Level 2 the main focus of our lives, we will tend to see life as a competition — constantly comparing ourselves to others and getting caught up in the "win, lose, or draw" game.

_____

_____

_____

_____

CRISIS 2

Sometimes people get stuck in the belief that their own egos are at the center of the universe. You may know someone like this. Let's imagine a guy named Brian who is just like any other normal teenager, but who falls for the Level 2 trap.

Brian tends to judge everyone in life by the "comparison game." He looks at the world in terms of "win, lose, or draw," and this brings out a lot of negative emotions.

The only thing that matters to Brian is winning, success, popularity, and control. Losing a competition, or some popularity, or control feels like losing his own identity. He becomes bitter and jealous at the successes of other people. He fears inferiority and begins to imagine that other people are laughing at him behind his back. He begins to hate himself.

If he believes in God, Brian will probably blame God for his failures. He will likely view God as a "Level 2 God" who doesn't care about him or his problems. That will make him angry at God, angry at other people, and depressed at his own sense of inferiority.

But winning brings its own problems. Since winning is what matters, Brian will become aggressively competitive to the point of running over other people. And it's not enough just to win once or twice; in order to continue appearing as if he were better than other people, and to prevent other people from overtaking his achievements, he constantly has to outdo everyone else, and even himself. He believes that if he doesn't keep doing better and better, people will stop caring or won't notice him anymore.

He can't stand being embarrassed in front of other people — especially people he thinks are inferior. If anybody challenges Brian, makes him look bad, or embarrasses him, he feels rage and gets that look described as "daggers in his eyes." He's likely to think about ways of "getting even."

Brian fears healthy relationships. He doesn't want to reveal too much about himself to others or they may begin to learn that he has weaknesses, and that would threaten his ego. In order to avoid that kind of closeness, he hides his true self and pumps himself up every chance he gets. Instead of looking for friends who really care about him, he looks for friends who admire him and whom he can control.

Eventually, most people get tired of being treated like Brian's footstool, so Brian either convinces himself that they're really just jealous of his superiority, or he becomes bitter towards people who won't grovel at his feet. He resents them, but he feels emptiness inside, like something is missing. He feels very lonely. Unfortunately, this is a hard feeling for him to overcome because, as a winner, he holds other people in contempt. This means that he looks at other people as if their lives are less significant than his, which makes people even less likely to want to be around Brian. And that leads him to even deeper resentment and loneliness.

Contempt: To look at other people as if their lives are less significant than ours.

At this point, Brian might think that the way out of this mess would be a draw. That's when he isn't really winning and he isn't really losing. He's just keeping his head above water—keeping up with the herd, so to speak.

Some people who are stuck on Level 2 will stay in the background out of a fear of losing. They protect their egos by not taking any risks, as a way of self-preservation. But they aren't going to find happiness in this, because they are still comparing themselves to everybody else. They are very self-conscious, and calculatingly aware of how they measure up. They feel like everyone is judging them. If somebody gets too close, asks too many questions, or shines a spotlight on them, they become anxious, nervous, shy, or suspicious. So drawing is not a way to escape the comparison game. They're stuck in the fear trap—fear about how they will measure up if they enter the game.

A person can feel any combination of the negative emotions of Crisis 2. It is not uncommon for one person to experience all three sets of emotions (win, lose, and draw) even within a day or two. Changes in life's circumstances and mood swings can push a person from one emotion to another.

Fortunately, there is a way to move beyond these negative emotions, and get out of Crisis 2. But in order to do it, we have to stop playing the comparison game.

Unfortunately, it's not easy to stop—especially if we've been playing for a long time, and comparing ourselves to those around us has become a habit. When Level 2 people suddenly try to stop, they often find themselves thinking, "Look at me! I'm no longer playing that dumb comparison game. I'm better than all those other losers who are still playing it." Of course, that's just another way of still playing. The way out is to replace the comparison game with something better. Setting our sights on something higher than Level 2 can keep Level 2 in check.

Remember that as you move through the four levels of happiness, each higher level becomes more intangible than the last one and more challenging to acquire. But most people find that the higher levels are also longer lasting and more deeply fulfilling than the lower ones.

HAPPINESS LEVEL 2: EGO-GRATIFICATION

CRISIS: RAGE, CONTEMPT, JEALOUSY, SUSPICION

NEGATIVE EMOTIONS OF THE LEVEL 2 COMPARISON GAME

WIN

Aggression
Rage
Has to keep doing better
Fears healthy relationships
Emptiness
Contempt
Resentment
Loneliness
Depression

LOSE

Loss of self-identity
Bitterness
Jealousy
Inferiority
Self-hatred
Blame
Anger
Depression

DRAW

Fear of losing
Fear of attention
Self-consciousness
Anxiety
Nervousness
Embarrassment
Suspicion
Overly-guarded

HAPPINESS 3

Have you ever heard the old saying, "If you're feeling down, do something nice for somebody"? There is wisdom in that statement. The most effective strategy for moving beyond the crisis of Level 2 is to look for the good beyond ourselves. Instead of worrying about how we measure up to everyone else, we can try to make a positive difference to others with our lives, time, energy, and talent. We all want to contribute to something bigger than ourselves. We all have a desire to make the world a better place, to help people, to be a part of what is good and not a part of what is evil. The fulfillment that comes from pursuing goodness or virtue is called Happiness 3.

Two ways that you can experience Level 3 are by doing good for others (doing for) and being with others in empathy (being with).

"Doing for" is the kind of happiness that comes from doing something that benefits somebody else — like helping another student understand a homework assignment, doing your brother's chores, letting others go first, creating something beautiful or useful, or sharing what you have with others. Anything we can do to make a positive difference with our lives can lead to a strong sense of fulfillment. When we do good works, we feel connected to something bigger than ourselves— something good and even noble.

But we don't actually have to be doing something to make a positive difference. Sometimes you can make a big difference simply by "being with" someone. When we spend time with other people and focus on them instead of on ourselves, we can experience what's called "empathy." "Empathy" means to feel what someone else is feeling. It's hard to do that if you don't spend time just being with other people. "Being with" is one of the most important aspects of an intimate relationship. If your best friend doesn't have time to spend with you, she's probably not going to be your best friend for long. Most marriages in which the spouses hardly see each other lack the depth necessary to be strong and healthy.

We can experience a "being with" type of empathy by things like putting an arm around a friend who is troubled, listening attentively to the story of an elderly person, smiling and acknowledging the homeless person on the street, playing a silly game with a small child, or watching the stars with our parents.

Empathy means to feel what someone else is feeling.

Focusing on Level 3 helps to keep Happiness 2 in check. When Brian was living for Level 2 as an end in itself (as his highest priority) he had to hide his true self, run over other people, be suspicious of them, and show that everyone else was inferior to him in order to find his meaning and identity. But in Level 3, this doesn't make any sense. We can't make a positive difference to somebody by running her over. So, if what we really want is Level 3, we have to be very careful not to let our competitive instincts come before what is good for other people.

For example, imagine Brian has a change of heart. In Level 3, if getting the highest grade in class means that Brian has to cheat off of Louise's paper, he'd rather settle for a lower

© Yuri_Arcurs / iStockphoto

LEVEL 3 BEHAVIOR
+ LEVEL 2 INTENTION
= LEVEL 2 HAPPINESS

LEVEL 3 BEHAVIOR
+ LEVEL 3 INTENTION
= LEVEL 3 HAPPINESS

grade. If being popular means he has to insult less popular people, he'll find another group of friends to hang around with. If showing that he is powerful means he has to beat up somebody who is weaker than he is, he'll give up the appearance of power and let people think what they want to think. In other words, when Level 3 is Brian's goal, he is no longer dominated and controlled by the Level 2 myth that he's better than everyone else. It doesn't mean that he no longer wants to be successful, popular, or powerful. But it does mean that Brian is not willing to sacrifice the greater good for a short-term ego-trip, and that makes all the difference.

Here's another example. Imagine that a Level 2 guy named Omar is helping Taylor with her math homework. He has a crush on Taylor and wants to show her how smart he is. Suddenly, Eva, who has been listening in on their conversation, interrupts Omar and says, "Actually, you might want to try solving the equation this way. It's less confusing than the way Omar is explaining it..." As Eva begins to show Taylor an easier way to solve the math problem, Omar's ego-sensitivity

will perk up. He will likely become irritated and embarrassed by Eva's meddling. Omar wants to be the one to help Taylor, because he wants to show her how smart he is. But Eva is threatening his move.

Notice that Omar is not interested in what is good for Taylor. He is interested in how he appears. So he will probably either tell Eva to mind her own business, or find another way to give Eva the hint to stay out of it.

If Omar had been motivated by Level 3, and actually wanted Taylor to learn math for her own good and not so that he would look good, then he would have appreciated Eva's help and may have said something like, "Wow, I guess I learned something, too." Ironically, he probably would have impressed Taylor with his common cause attitude.

Common cause means to allow other people to share a common goal, rather than trying to grab all the glory for ourselves. The best leaders are the ones who have common cause attitudes.

Notice that Omar can be going through Level 3 motions (helping Taylor with her math problem) with a Level 2 intention (doing it so that he gets recognized or appreciated). But to get Level 3 happiness, we have to match up Level 3 *behavior* with Level 3 *intentions*.

We can experience Level 3 happiness even if other people don't appreciate the good that we are trying to do. Happiness is not just about being in a good mood or feeling like we want to laugh. Real happiness is about choosing goals in life that are truly worthy, and working on reaching those goals. It's about having meaning in life that is deep, fulfilling, and lasting. Sometimes, just knowing that we did the right thing can be enough to give life deeper meaning and purpose, even when others don't recognize or thank us.

This does not mean that gratitude and recognition are not important. Relationships cannot deepen and grow when the other person does not recognize the good that we do and express appreciation. So Level 3 people should work hard on having these virtues themselves.

WE CAN EXPERIENCE LEVEL 3 HAPPINESS EVEN IF OTHER PEOPLE DON'T APPRECIATE THE GOOD THAT WE ARE TRYING TO DO.

Three Characteristics of Happiness Level 3

1] **It is long term.** It lasts much longer than Levels 1 or 2. An experience of being there when somebody really needs us can change our entire lives. It can make us better people. The positive effect we have on others can multiply and change their lives for the long term, too.

2] **It requires a lot more from us.** Level 3 requires some self-sacrifice and uses more of our deeper human powers, like love, empathy, kindness, generosity, patience, humility, and forgiveness. These powers are a deeper part of us than Level 1 and 2 powers, so they are much more deeply fulfilling.

3] **It extends farther beyond ourselves to include others.** In Level 3, we want to make the biggest possible difference with our lives, time, energy, and talent. If given the opportunity, we can help do good for our school, neighborhood, church, community, culture, and sometimes even the whole world. We can make a difference to people we don't know and have never met.

Level 3 is so deeply satisfying that you may think there couldn't be anything better than this. Unfortunately, no sooner do we awaken the Level 3 powers within us, then crisis creeps in once again.

CRISIS 3

What's the last movie you watched in which the hero defeated the bad guys, saved the day, won his true love's heart, and lived happily ever after? There are a lot of great movies like that, and they're fun to watch because we identify with the hero and feel triumphant when good conquers evil.

Unfortunately, as soon as the movie is over and the news comes on, you see that the world is still filled with evil, broken hearts, sadness, and death. The biggest problem with Level 3 is that human beings want to overcome all evil, sadness, broken-heartedness, and death – but we aren't able to do it on our own as human beings. We aren't powerful enough. And so we get frustrated and cynical, and begin to lose hope.

Philosophers have recognized for thousands of years that human beings don't just desire *some* good in the world. We are built to desire *ultimate* good. Human beings want what is infinite, eternal, absolute, unconditional, and perfect. We seek absolute truth, unconditional love, perfect justice, perfect beauty, and perfect unity.

Unconditional = Complete or guaranteed. Without conditions, limitations, or strings attached.

For example, most people find it unjust that some of us have our basic survival needs met, but others don't. We want to stamp out *all* injustice wherever it exists. Most people are not satisfied when they see some families who love each other, but others who are struggling with division, violence, or conflict. We want to see *all* families living in harmony and unity. Most people are not satisfied with the current level of knowledge we have about the world. We want to know *everything* there is to know about the world, and use that knowledge to make life better for ourselves and others.

Think about the last time someone lied to you or did not love you in an authentic way. Think about when someone treated you unfairly, or when your family or friends didn't understand you and you felt like an outsider. Were you satisfied? Or did you feel like something wasn't right?

The ancient Greek philosopher Plato noticed 2,400 years ago that all human beings seem to have a built-in desire for perfection in these five areas: truth, love, justice, beauty, and unity. His followers called these five areas the "five transcendentals," because they transcend (go beyond) physical reality. They go beyond what we can see, taste, touch, hear, and smell. We can know more about truth, love, justice, beauty, and unity with our hearts than we can with our five senses. Because these five transcendentals play such an important role in the search for human happiness, we will go through each one to see where the crisis lies, and then we'll explore them more deeply in the section on Happiness Level 4.

Transcendent means "beyond physical." It's something that is really real, but we cannot see, taste, touch, hear, or smell it. Examples would be love, truth, or justice.

© Sean Boggs / iStockphoto

THE DESIRE FOR ABSOLUTE TRUTH

Truth is important to Level 3 people because it is necessary in order to make a positive difference in the world. For example, when scientists find out the truth about certain diseases, they can use that knowledge to find cures and vaccines.

But human beings don't just want some truth. We want absolute truth. If you've ever been around a small child, you know that they have an infinite supply of questions and are often unsatisfied with the answers you give them. They will keep asking you question after question until you throw up your hands and say, "Time out! Let's go play with your toys."

Maybe you've even had the experience of asking someone a series of questions, but you don't seem to be getting the answers that satisfy your concerns. You keep prodding with more questions until the person finally responds, "Well, that's just the way it is." You probably didn't feel very satisfied with this answer. This sense of dissatisfaction is a clue that, as human beings, we recognize the inadequacy of incomplete truth and will never stop asking questions until we get all the right answers to all the questions that could be asked.

Have you ever noticed that animals do not seem to do this? For example, cats have knowledge about many biological opportunities and dangers. But they have not advanced their condition over the last 300,000 years. They're still doing essentially the same things that they have always done.

When animals run out of biological opportunities (such as being fed or being petted) and dangers (such as avoiding predators), they fall asleep. When human beings run out of biological opportunities and dangers, they start asking questions—about how the world works, about themselves and other people, about the meaning of life and right versus wrong, etc. These questions lead to genuine creativity, to advances in knowledge, and advances in the human condition. Human beings seem to be the only creatures on earth that possess the ability to

> **THE HUMAN PURSUIT OF TRUTH CAN LEAD TO A CRISIS.**

ask questions and use each answer to continuously advance their own condition.

But many philosophers and psychologists have noticed that the human pursuit of truth can lead to a crisis. Every question we ask opens the door to other questions, and the more questions we answer, the more we realize how little we actually know. This can lead to frustration, cynicism, and even despair as some people begin to believe that there is no such thing as truth, or that truth is just an illusion.

There are many examples of brilliant men and women who tried to find truth in philosophy, science, and mathematics, but there always seemed to be some unanswered question that got in their way. The frustration that comes from this roadblock can cause people to despair of ever finding the truth, and can cause intelligent people to defend flawed theories even when their reasoning or their science has been disproven.

THE DESIRE FOR UNCONDITIONAL LOVE

Love means to desire what is good for someone else so much that it becomes easier to do good for that other person than it is to do good for yourself.

That is a very different notion of love than what we are used to hearing in music, on television, and on the internet. Real love means being connected to other human beings by the way you care about them, by giving your self and your time to them as a gift, by being concerned about their needs, and by accepting their special, unique, and valuable personhood.

Love is important to Level 3 people because we cannot make a positive difference to others if we do not love them. But human beings seem to go beyond their own limited ability to love. We seem to have a sense of what perfect and unconditional love ought to be like.

The good news is that our sense of perfect love drives us to want to be more and more perfectly and unconditionally loving towards others. The bad news is that it can cause us to expect ever more perfect love from

© Kemter / iStockphoto

LOVE IS TO DESIRE THE GOOD FOR SOMEONE ELSE SO MUCH THAT IT BECOMES EASIER TO DO GOOD FOR THAT OTHER PERSON THAN IT IS TO DO GOOD FOR YOURSELF.

An example would be when a new mother and father desperately need to get some sleep, but they get out of bed at two in the morning to tend to the needs of their crying baby. Share your stories of similar experiences of love at www.principlesandchoices.com.

ourselves and from others—an expectation that will quickly become impossible to fulfill. Since we are human and imperfect, this unreasonable expectation will be crushed when we realize that neither we nor others can fulfill our desire for perfect and unconditional love. We all have faults and struggle with seeing and understanding one another. We can be selfish – putting ourselves above the needs of others.

Here is an example of the crisis that can happen with love in Level 3. A girl meets a boy and falls in love. She thinks to herself, "He will make all my dreams come true. He is my one true love." She sees only the good in him. He's good looking, smart, funny, and cheerful.

But then, one day, he begins to show signs of imperfection. He's not always there when she needs him. He forgets about important dates, like her birthday. He sometimes doesn't understand her. She discovers that he's not actually perfectly humble, gentle, kind, forgiving, compassionate, and concerned about her every need. She becomes irritated, frustrated, and then crushed. She thinks, "I can't believe I thought he was really THE ONE." Of course, he wasn't THE ONE, because he's not perfect and never will be. Nevertheless, she is hurt inside. She expected him to be perfect and he wasn't; so she begins to make demands on him to be more perfect, which, of course, he can't fulfill. When he is unable to be perfectly loving toward her in every way, she starts to think about ending the relationship.

This is one of the biggest reasons why romantic relationships and marriages fall apart. Relationship experts warn us to avoid the pitfall of expecting the people we love to be perfect. It will lead to irritation, frustration, dashed expectations, hurt feelings, and broken relationships. Of course, we should expect the people who love us to be gentle and kind, forgiving and caring, compassionate and generous, and to be concerned about us and what is good for us. But the problem lies in expecting other people to be *perfectly* loving, and giving them no room for error or growth.

To sum up, the crisis with love in Level 3 is that we will always *desire* perfect love, but our ability to *actually* love is imperfect. Many people who put human love on a pedestal and expect it to be perfect become cynical when they discover that some of their greatest heroes have fallen short of perfect love. Some people can become so disillusioned that they begin to believe that there is no such thing as perfect and unconditional love.

THE DESIRE FOR PERFECT JUSTICE

Justice is defined as "giving someone his due" or "giving someone what she is owed." We all seem to have a sense of good and evil. Many researchers have discovered a shared sense of what is good and what is evil between people of all ages, eras, cultures, and nations. Most people seem to know that murder is evil, and that sharing what we have with those who are less fortunate is good. Most of us have a strong awareness of something being wrong when we cooperate with evil. We feel guilty, ashamed, inauthentic, and remorseful. We also have a strong awareness when we cooperate with good. We feel noble, honorable, courageous, and proud.

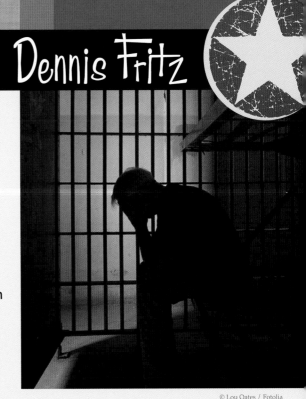

I n 2006, the famous novelist John Grisham wrote a book called, *The Innocent Man: Murder and Injustice in a Small Town*. It relates the true story of Dennis Fritz, a high school science teacher and single father who went to prison for the murder of a waitress at a nightclub in 1982.

Eventually, advanced DNA testing proved that Dennis Fritz was innocent, and he was released after spending 12 years in prison for a crime he didn't commit.

When he was later interviewed on television, Mr. Fritz said, "The harm that it did to me was that it took 12 years out of my life, away from my family members. I was cheated of watching my daughter grow and flower into a woman. No amount of money on the face of the earth could even begin to make an amend for what happened."

© Lou Oates / Fotolia

THOUGHTS TO PONDER...

> What injustices do you see in this story?

> What thoughts would go through your head if this happened to you?

> Read Dennis' comment in the last sentence of the story. If justice means "giving people what they are owed," do you think it is possible for Dennis to receive perfect justice in this world? Does it sound to you like Dennis wants perfect justice?

> Regardless of whether you believe it exists, do you *desire* perfect justice for Dennis? If so, could your desire be pointing to something real that could satisfy the desire? Is it possible to have a desire that can never be fulfilled? If so, where is the desire coming from?

Even more than this, we seem to have a sense of what perfect and absolute justice and goodness would be like. For many people, it is not enough to simply avoid evil in our own lives. Most people are deeply concerned about the evil that occurs in other parts of the world as well. History is filled with examples of people trying to fight every kind of oppression, injustice, and inequity—even for people they have never met, and for future generations they will never know.

Justice is very important to Level 3 people because it makes a positive difference in the world. But crisis happens when we begin to *expect* perfect justice in an imperfect world.

A human being's natural state is to want perfect justice. Think about how many times you have heard small children yell, "That's not fair!" They seem to have a built-in knowledge of what perfect justice is, and they are very aware of when they are not getting it.

A HUMAN BEING'S NATURAL STATE IS TO WANT PERFECT JUSTICE.

Teenagers and adults do the same thing. We have a sense of what perfect justice ought to be, and we believe others ought to agree. When our sense of perfect justice has been violated, we are in a state of shock. We really expect that perfect justice ought to happen, and when it doesn't, it disappoints us so deeply that it can consume us.

Of course, there's good news and bad news to our sense of perfect justice. On the one hand, it can bring people together and cause us to work harder for justice in the world. On the other hand, it can also cause us to expect perfect justice from an imperfect world that cannot deliver. This will cause crushed expectations, frustration, and disappointment, which can eventually turn into outrage, impatience, judging others, and even cynicism and despair. We may think to ourselves, "Human beings are just rotten at heart, and they'll cheat you any chance they get." Sometimes when people get older and have seen or experienced significant injustice that has not been corrected, they can become negative and believe that there is no such thing as true justice.

THE DESIRE FOR PERFECT BEAUTY

If you are like most people, you probably spend some time thinking about your appearance. Maybe you wish you had clear skin, a good figure, and fashionable clothes. You might be concerned about your muscular build, your complexion, or whether your hairstyle is keeping up with trends. We all want to be attractive to others. Another word for that is "beautiful." When you think of "beautiful," do you think about a famous movie star? A model? An athlete? The latest fashions?

Now think a little more deeply. What about nature? Think about a prairie scene in the springtime, a sunset over the mountains, the ocean shore in the morning. Is that different? What is it that makes the mountain or the ocean beautiful? Let's go a little deeper. Think about music, art, and architecture. The notes, the chords, the colors,

the arches. When we hear beautiful music, or see a beautiful work of art or a stunning cathedral, we often feel a certain "rapture" or "ecstasy" which has an addictive quality. But what is it that makes beauty beautiful?

There's something about the harmony of form that makes us feel at peace. If you visit the scene of a major volcanic eruption where all the plants have been blown away, the trees are stripped into skeletal toothpicks, the lake is a steaming mass of putrid muck, and all the animals have either been incinerated or chased away, you probably wouldn't think, "What a beautiful place. I should like to live here some day." But if you visit the valley of a mountain where birds are singing, flowers are in bloom, a river is bubbling nearby, and there is a view of a waterfall in the distance, you may find yourself feeling at home, and dream about how pleasant it would be to stay for a while.

The harmony of form also stirs up our hearts. When you listen to music that is loud, out of tune, distorted, and makes you want to bang your head against a wall and let out a primal scream, it may be exciting and even fun, but you probably aren't thinking to yourself, "That is the most beautiful, peaceful music I have ever heard, and I hope they play it for me when I am dying." On the other hand, when you listen to the melody and harmony of a Brahms symphony, you might find yourself in ecstasy, your heart rising in your chest, and maybe even tears welling up in your eyes.

The harmony of form can even lift our souls. If you passed by a sewage treatment plant made out of unfinished gray concrete, no windows, and a tangle of pipes and ducts tunneling in and out of the building, you would probably hold your nose and just keep walking. But if you passed by a towering cathedral with uniform domes, majestic pillars, interweaving arches, glorious stained glass windows, and ornate carvings, statues, and doors, you would probably stop in your tracks and stand in awe, trying to take it all in at once.

Almost all human beings seem to have a common sense of "the beautiful" through an appreciation of forms that harmonize, that have unity, and

that fit together. But human beings don't just desire *some* beauty. We seem to want *perfect* beauty. We want to see, hear, and experience beauty in its purest, most perfect form.

Unfortunately, this is quite difficult to achieve. We only need to look at daily life to notice our disappointment with nearly every form of human and natural beauty. The bride who has just finished paying for the alterations on her wedding dress notices another dress on the rack that is even more beautiful than the one she already bought. The man sitting in the cathedral finds that it is nice, but parts of it are overdone or not quite right. The woman listening to the Brahms symphony thinks that it is lovely, but it goes on too long in some places, and after listening to it too many times, she gets bored. The hikers admiring the nature scene are in awe of the sunset, but there are too many mosquitoes.

We can see frustration with the imperfection of natural beauty when we read the biographies of great artists, musicians, and poets. So many of their lives were filled with tragedy as these gifted men and women poured themselves into their art and never felt that it reached perfection. There are many stories of artists who became depressed or mentally ill, and in some cases even abused themselves because they could not perfectly recreate the perfect beauty that they sensed in their hearts and souls.

Beauty is important to Level 3 people because it brings a sense of awe, inspiration, and hope into the world. But crisis can occur when human beings idolize natural beauty and try to get perfect beauty out of a

world that has imperfect building blocks and imperfect artists. On the positive side, our desire for complete beauty causes us to strive toward creating more and more beautiful art, music, and architecture. But on the negative side, when we never quite reach perfection, we can become deeply dissatisfied, frustrated, disillusioned, bored, and restless.

THE DESIRE FOR PERFECT UNITY

If you type "feel like an outsider" in a search engine, you'll get over a million hits. It is a very common feeling. In one online article, the author writes:

> I spent a lot of my life feeling like an outsider. The good news is that we're in very good company. In reading autobiographies of some of the most famous people, one of the statements you'll commonly see is, "I felt like an outsider." People like Nicole Kidman, Anthony Hopkins, Walt Disney, and Maria Shriver are just a few. Even Tom Cruise was teased as a child because he had dyslexia and so felt he didn't fit in.[B]

Human beings want to feel that we are at harmony with all that is. We want to feel that we belong in the universe, that we are at home in the cosmos, that we are at peace with everything that exists. Philosophers sometimes call this the desire for perfect unity.

Have you ever been in class, in the cafeteria, or at a school dance or other social event, and felt like you didn't

© reflektastudios / Fotolia

WHAT WOULD IT FEEL LIKE TO BE AT PEACE WITH EVERYTHING AND EVERYONE?

belong? Maybe your best friends or family members were there and people were laughing and enjoying themselves, but somehow you felt out of kilter with everything, like something was missing or off-balance. Maybe you were even in your own home but you felt awkward, different, or out of place. You might have felt misunderstood or sensed an emptiness or lack of peace, but couldn't really put your finger on anything specific to explain it. You felt alienated, like you weren't at home in the universe.

Many philosophers and theologians tell us that this feeling indicates that human beings seem to have an awareness of what perfect home (also called "perfect unity") should be like. The good news is that this awareness causes us to work hard at building

CRISIS 3 OCCURS WHEN OUR SEARCH FOR PERFECTION IN AN IMPERFECT WORLD LEAVES US FRUSTRATED, UNSATISFIED, AND DISAPPOINTED.

communities, friendships, and stronger families—which are all Level 3 ideals. Our culture is very focused on being inclusive and welcoming to diverse groups of people. Many people dedicate their lives to bringing about world peace, or resolving conflicts at home or in other nations.

The bad news is that our inability to achieve world peace, or even to achieve perfect peace within our families or our own souls can make us feel confused, empty, frustrated, and lost. Feeling like an outsider can lead to listlessness and depression, which can cause us to blame other people for not helping us to belong. The news media is filled with tragic stories about people who joined violent gangs, mobs, or even terrorist organizations because of an unfulfilled desire to fit in.

SUMMARY OF CRISIS 3

As the last five sections show, Level 3 can lead to a serious crisis. The problem is that human beings *want* perfect truth, love, justice, beauty, and unity, but we sometimes try to *satisfy* this desire with imperfect people and things in an imperfect world. It seems that when we try to make the world bring us perfect happiness, we become disappointed and frustrated with the imperfections and limitations of the world.

When people make Level 3 their highest goal in life, they often complain of being dissatisfied and disappointed. When they cannot get perfection from this world, Level 3 people will sometimes become cynical, believing that life is all about wanting something that they can never have. They may eventually give up trying altogether—continuing to feel unsatisfied and disillusioned. This can be referred to as Crisis 3.

What is the answer?

Some people feel that life is completely absurd, and we will forever desire what we cannot ever have. But that idea has led many great thinkers to ask a series of important questions, such as: "If perfect truth, love, justice, beauty, and unity do not exist, then how did we get an awareness of them? How can we be aware of something that doesn't exist? How can so many people be dissatisfied with imperfection if there is no such thing as perfection to compare it to? Dogs don't seem to care about perfect truth, or love, or justice. Chimpanzees don't seem to worry about finding perfect beauty or unity. Why do human beings care so much?

If you find yourself intrigued by these questions, the next section will discuss the ways in which many people have answered these questions throughout history.

HAPPINESS LEVEL 3: CONTRIBUTION TO OTHERS
CRISIS: FRUSTRATION AND CRUSHED EXPECTATIONS

© Alexey Klementiev / Fotolia

HAPPINESS 4

Millions of people have recorded their experience of finding happiness through belief in God. You can find literally millions of such recorded experiences in books, videos, websites, journals, songs, poems, letters, interviews, social media, films, plays, speeches, and other works. Some of them talk about God as being absolute Truth, unconditional Love, perfect Justice, perfect Beauty, or perfect Unity. Their journey led them to an intense awareness that God is all of these things and wants to share Himself with us. And that belief led them to a deep and lasting peace.

This spiritual peace is so profound and complete for those who experience it that it doesn't have the crisis of Level 3. There is an acceptance that human beings and the things of this world cannot satisfy their desire for perfect happiness. They don't deny that they have this desire for perfection, but rather than looking to fulfill it with other people, they look to fulfill it with God. That is what helps them avoid the pitfalls of Level 3. Because

of that, this kind of happiness needs its own category – Happiness Level 4.

There are some significant differences between Happiness 4 and the other three kinds of happiness. Level 4 goes beyond the first three levels because it is eternal. In other words, if God exists, and if He can make you perfectly happy, the happiness would have to be eternal – meaning that it will last forever.

Level 4 also requires total surrender. This is important to a Level 4 person, because without surrendering to God, he or she runs the risk of clinging to imperfect things and people as ultimate meaning and purpose in life. In this view, putting things ahead of God will cause a conflict with the desire for perfect Truth, Love, Justice, Beauty, and Unity. Since the desire for perfection does not go away, one will try to make those imperfect things and people become one's god, and will try to make them satisfy the need for perfection.

By nature, Level 4 is accessible by all people in all generations and from all cultures, regardless of their circumstances. Recall that Level 1 does

My Life is an inspirational movie starring Michael Keaton and Nicole Kidman, which tells the story of a man who journeys through all four levels of happiness. Use code **PCS114** for a synopsis and commentary on this movie.

© DNY59 / iStockphoto

not extend beyond yourself at all. It affects only you. It is possible for Level 2 to positively affect people around you who might share in your success or popularity. And Level 3 can positively affect many people who benefit from your acts of goodness and love. But Level 4 extends infinitely beyond yourself. If God is perfect and unlimited, then He would be able to fulfill the ultimate desires of any and all human beings, with all their differences and their special and unique characteristics.

Furthermore, people who seek Level 4 report finding greater happiness when they work to help others achieve Level 4 happiness as well. Level 4 motivates them to want to evangelize other people and other nations. It motivates them to pray for others. In Level 3, there are only a limited number of people that one can reach. But because God is unlimited, individuals who seek Level 4 can use prayer to ask God to extend their good acts and intentions to affect every person in the world. If God is real, He would have the power to do so.

Three Characteristics of Happiness Level 4

1] **It is eternal** and can bring eternal happiness.

2] **It requires surrender** to perfect Truth, Love, Justice, Beauty, and Unity (God).

3] **It can affect all people** from all generations, nations, and cultures.

People have struggled with beliefs about God since the beginning of recorded history. It isn't the purpose of this book to explore specific religious beliefs or traditions. But the inquiry into human meaning and purpose should include a thorough look at the major questions surrounding this level of happiness.

When students explore Happiness Level 4, they usually ask three major questions: 1] Can we prove that God exists? 2] Can God fulfill all of our five transcendental desires? and 3] Does God want to be with us for all eternity? The following three sections will address these questions and offer some philosophical reflection.

QUESTION #1: CAN WE PROVE THAT GOD EXISTS?

We often hear that we cannot prove God exists, because we cannot see Him or detect His presence with a scientific instrument. While it is true that one cannot scientifically prove God's existence (because if He were real, God would have no boundaries that would allow science to physically detect His presence), science *can* provide evidence that points to the existence of God.

For example, many biologists argue that the human eye is so complex that it is virtually impossible for it to have evolved into existence randomly, without the guiding hand of a super-intelligent power.

Furthermore, many philosophers have used reason and logic to prove the existence of God. If you are interested in logical proofs, use the code in the sidebar of this page, and scroll to Units D-G. We have included a simple form of one logical proof for God's existence in Appendix 1 at the end of this book.

QUESTION #2: CAN GOD FULFILL ALL OF OUR HIGHEST DESIRES?

There is extensive evidence for God's existence in every field of science. But science cannot provide any evidence for what God is like. Science cannot tell us whether God can fulfill all of our desires. It cannot tell us whether He is good or evil, patient or impatient, forgiving or condemning. Science does not provide any insight about whether God wants to be with us or would rather be left alone.

To answer these questions, we must once again turn to philosophy and to the logic of our minds and hearts. If we can reasonably conclude that God is absolute Truth, unconditional Love, perfect Justice, perfect Beauty, and perfect Unity, then we would have strong evidence that He can and will fulfill our highest desires. Appendix 2 offers philosophical evidence for this.

QUESTION #3: DOES GOD WANT TO BE WITH US FOR ALL ETERNITY?

If you have read Appendices 1 and 2, you may find that there is reasonable evidence that God exists, and evidence that He can fulfill all of our highest desires. But this leads many students to wonder, "Is God just some big, untouchable, unknowable goodness out there in the heavens, floating around, being perfect Truth, Love, Justice, Beauty, and Unity all by Himself? Or is He actually a Person who wants to be with us eternally, and wants to fulfill all our desires for perfect Truth, Love, Justice, Beauty, and Unity?"

In order to answer this question, we can put together some of what we've already learned, to do a little thought experiment. Here are five questions to think about. Consider each one carefully before you proceed to the next.

Thought #1: What do you want more than anything else in the world? What do you really desire the most, down in the depths of your heart and soul? Is it love?

Thought #2: If what you want is to be loved, wouldn't God, who is perfect, have to have love as a part of His nature? (If you answer, "No, He would not have to contain love as part of His

★ Think of ways in which a lower level of happiness could come into conflict with each of the five transcendentals in Happiness 4.

_____
_____
_____
_____
_____
_____
_____
_____
_____
_____
_____
_____
_____
_____
_____
_____
_____
_____
_____
_____
_____
_____
_____
_____

nature," then wouldn't God be missing the greatest virtue, and therefore be less perfect than we are?)

Thought #3: If love is a part of God's nature, then would God, who has no limitations, be able to love you unconditionally? (If you answer, "No, He would not be able to love me unconditionally," wouldn't that mean that God's love is limited, and so He isn't really God?)

Thought #4: If God loves you unconditionally, would He want to be with you for all eternity? (If you answer, "No, He does not want to be with me for all eternity," then would God's love really be unconditional?)

Thought #5: If God wants to be with you for all eternity, but you cannot get to Him by yourself because you are limited and He is unlimited; you are finite and He is infinite; you are imperfect and He is perfect; then would God be willing to come to you?

This thought experiment suggests that God wants to be with us for all eternity. And it also indicates that He would be willing to come to us, rather than watching us try in vain to come to Him. He would be like a gentle and loving parent who would do anything to help us be with Him — even if it meant coming to earth to become one of us. Even if it meant suffering and dying for us.

"Behold, a virgin shall conceive and bear a son, and his name shall be called 'Emmanuel,' which means 'God with us.'"

(Matthew 1:23)

Choosing Level 4 does not require a person to ignore the other levels of happiness. If the lower levels come into conflict with one's relationship with God, a Level 4 person will try to prioritize Level 4 and will work to ensure that the other three levels are pursued in ways that don't cause conflict.

This means that Level 4 people do not have to stop loving their family and friends in order to pursue God. From a Level 4 perspective, God wants us to continually learn to increase in love for other people. Our ability to grow in love for others is unlimited. But God would not want us to try to force human beings to fulfill our desire for perfect Love, because they would never be able to do that. Only God can do that. From a Level 4 perspective, the more we love God, the more we will be able to love other people. Why? Because love for God would increase our knowledge about God, and therefore our knowledge about love – about compassion, generosity, kindness, self-sacrifice, patience, gentleness, faithfulness, humble-heartedness, and forgiveness.

Viktor Frankl was an Austrian neurologist and psychiatrist who lived from 1905–1997. Because they were Jews, he and his wife and parents were imprisoned in various concentration camps during the Nazi Holocaust. His wife and parents were killed, but Dr. Frankl survived and was liberated in 1945. He later wrote a book called *Man's Search for Meaning*.

Attribution: Bundesarchiv, Bild 183-B12274 / CC-BY-SA

In his book, Viktor Frankl explains the importance of how we define meaning in life. While in the concentration camps, he noticed that some prisoners were entirely focused on their own immediate problems: how to get food, how to avoid a beating, how to keep warm, and when they were going to be liberated. Focusing on their own needs became the sole meaning and purpose in life for many of the prisoners.

On the other hand, there were some prisoners who held tightly to a deep spiritual life, and tended to focus more on the needs of others. They struggled with forgiving those who were persecuting them. They looked for opportunities to help other prisoners with acts of kindness. Dr. Frankl speaks of one man who asked God to take his own suffering and death and use it to allow his loved ones to escape the same fate.

The remarkable thing is that most of the prisoners who focused on themselves eventually lost hope and gave up. Many of them died from despair. But the prisoners who found meaning in something greater than themselves—in a spiritual life of forgiveness and love—survived in far greater numbers.

When Viktor Frankl was liberated from the prison camp, he developed a method of psychotherapy called "logotherapy," which means "meaning therapy." In this type of therapy, a psychotherapist helps the patient find happiness by looking for deeper meaning in life. Dr. Frankl learned that how we define "meaning in life" makes all the difference in the world to our happiness, well being, and even survival. If we were to translate Dr. Frankl's findings into the language of this chapter, we might say that the key to real happiness, even in the face of tremendous suffering, is to define our meaning not by Levels 1 and 2, but by Levels 3 and 4.

Photo: Tiago Fioreze

Use code **PCS116** to access vocabulary and other study tools for this chapter.

CRISIS 4

Crisis 4 occurs when one believes that God exists and that perfect happiness is His love, but one runs away from Him and doesn't let Him in. This might occur because someone has done something she believes cannot be forgiven, or because she thinks that God is so mighty He wouldn't want to be with her, or perhaps another reason.

One way to solve this crisis is to think about the following: If God cannot or will not forgive us, or if He does not want to be with us because He thinks we are too insignificant, then He is not unconditionally forgiving and He is not unconditionally loving. If that were true, then He would not be perfect. He would be limited by His own ego. But if God were imperfect and limited, then He couldn't really be God. He would just be another imperfect creature like us. So if you have belief that God exists, then you really have to consider that God can and will forgive anything, and that He can and does want to be with you forever. Accepting this truth is only possible if you are willing to talk to God through prayer, listen to Him in your heart, and respond to Him with trust.

You can avoid Crisis 4 if you practice humble surrender to God's love through prayer, and allow Him to come to you. God can and will help you let go of the false idols from Happiness Levels 1, 2, and 3 that may be preventing you from seeing and achieving real joy, peace, and freedom. It takes a lot of humility and trust to let God do all that for you. It takes a lot of faith to believe that He would care about you that much, and would want to be with you in total unconditional love, with all your faults and failings. But it is what He wants to do. Would you expect a real God to be any less than this?

If you trust God to fill every aspect of your life and heart, if you are willing to hold nothing back from Him, if you are humble enough to let Him in to even the darkest and least attractive corners of your life, He will not let you down. He will not abandon you. He will not disappoint you. Of course, you will still slip up from time to time—you are, after all, only human. But God will still be there, and He will always help you get back on track. The happiness you will find from always letting Him help you will be far greater, far deeper, far more fulfilling and transformative, and much longer lasting than any other type of happiness. It will look and feel exactly like what you have been longing for.

IF GOD DOES NOT LOVE YOU, CAN HE REALLY BE GOD?

© Sam Burt Photography / iStockphoto

IT'S YOUR CHOICE

The four levels of happiness laid out in this chapter are based on the observations of hundreds of great minds over thousands of years, and are reflected in every form of art, music, drama, and literature. They are also seen in the teachings of the world's greatest religions.

Ultimately, however, each one of us must make our own choice about what we believe will lead to happiness, and what we will choose as our highest priority in life. This is a very personal decision which no one can make for you. Here, we presented you with a model. To verify whether our model is correct, you will have to test it yourself. If you find that physical pleasure and ego-gratification do not leave you ultimately fulfilled, we encourage you to try Levels 3 and 4 to see whether they can offer greater meaning and purpose.

You may have questions or objections to this chapter. Many questions have been asked by other students. We have answered the most frequent ones on our website. Use code **PCS113** to read our answers, and feel free to dialogue with us by submitting your own questions and thoughts.

Level 4 and Jesus Christ

The section on Level 4 in this chapter discussed how happiness is fulfilled through a relationship with God and surrender to His unconditional Love.

Although it goes beyond the purpose of this book, that relationship is made concrete through a relationship with Jesus in the Church. We encourage you to speak with your pastor or the chaplain of your school to learn how to grow in a deeper knowledge and love of Jesus Christ and His Church. You can also use code **PCS136** to read two short, thought-provoking articles about God's unique and personal love for you, and His invitation for you to respond to His love.

CHAPTER 2: SUCCESS AND QUALITY OF LIFE

Imagine you have graduated from high school. You get married, have two children, live in a modest, yellow, three-bedroom home, and land a decent job that pays the bills. You are a good person—loving, generous, humble, and honest. You're happy.

One day you are walking down the street when a young man stops you, gives you his business card, and says, "Wow, you have the most interesting face. I am a movie producer from Hollywood, and I just happen to be making a movie where we need a face like yours. How would you like to be famous?" You go with him, make the movie, and suddenly your name is a household word. You start getting so many calls from movie producers that you have to hire an agent. You become famous. And then you become rich.

Deciding that you ought to set your sights a little higher, you spend a million dollars on a campaign for Congress, and you win. Four years later, you become the President of the United States. You are the leader of the free world. You can meet anyone you want. You can buy anything you want, and everyone knows who you are. You have tremendous power and influence, and are living a life of great success and quality.

Or are you?

One night when it's really late, you wake up and find that you can't get back to sleep. You get out of your presidential bed, turn on the television set, and flip to a late night movie. It's a story about a person who works a dull job to pay the bills, until one day a chance encounter happens with a movie producer, and everything changes. Fame... money... power... influence.

Unfortunately, as the movie progresses, the main character slowly loses sight of virtues like love, generosity, humility, and honesty. Those virtues were useful once upon a time. But now they seem weak, like obstacles that just slow down progress toward success. The character learns to get ahead much faster by being self-absorbed, stingy, proud, and dishonest.

© ISO3000 / iStockphoto

Eventually, the character gets divorced, becomes alcoholic and overweight, and struggles with bitterness and depression. The children have grown up and never come to visit anymore. Old friends stopped calling years ago. Holidays have become boring. Home seems a distant memory. God is no longer important. Everything was sacrificed for fame... money... power... influence. Extreme loneliness has left an empty hole where happiness used to be. Despair sets in, soon followed by thoughts of suicide.

Suddenly, the camera zooms in on the face of the main character. The actor's eyes are staring right at you through the television set. As you stare back, you realize that it's your own eyes you are seeing. The movie is about you. Someone has made a movie about your life.

Furious, you pick up the phone and call the White House operator, but there's no answer. You pop your head out the door and look down the long hallway. No Secret Service. That's odd. You step outside. No sounds. You walk down the street. No traffic. Nothing. Where is everybody? You're confused and your head is hurting, so you sit down on the curb.

At that moment, an old man sits down next to you and hands you a business card which contains only one word: "God." You're shocked.

"Is this some kind of joke?" you ask. "You're God?" He nods. "Am I dead?" He nods again. "Well, where is everybody?" God points to a building down the street. It is a modest, yellow, three-bedroom home. Inside is your spouse, your children, and all your old friends. There's music and laughter. Everyone there is happy. God smiles at you and starts to walk toward the house. But you don't follow.

"Wait a minute," you say. "I'm not going in there. I gave up that old place a long time ago. I worked hard to become successful. I'm a famous, rich, powerful, and influential person. I think I deserve a little higher quality of life than that old dump."

God looks at you with deep sadness in His eyes, but you are insistent. So He points to the other side of the street. There you see a magnificent golden castle. "That's more like it," you say.

You run up the street to the house, open the door, and peer inside. It's wonderful. It's better than anything you could have ever imagined. It's more delightful than your wildest dreams. But then, before you step inside, you notice something. There are no people inside. No life. Nobody. It's just you. You are completely alone.

How does this story end?

How do you define success?

DOES SUCCESS MEAN HAVING A LOT OF MONEY OR BEING BETTER THAN EVERYONE ELSE? HOW DO YOU DEFINE QUALITY OF LIFE? DOES IT MEAN ENJOYING FINE THINGS, GOOD HEALTH, OR THE ADMIRATION OF OTHERS?

When you compare a movie star, a famous model, or an award-winning singer to an old, poor, homeless man, who do you think is most successful? Who would you say has the higher quality of life?

Think about it this way: What if the movie star was alcoholic, depressed, had no real friendships, and was angry at God? What if the singer was on drugs, addicted to pornography, and suicidal? Would you think these people were "successful"? What if the elderly homeless man spent his time in the park entertaining children with card tricks, felt loved by God, and always had a smile for everyone? Would you think his life was a failure?

Nearly everyone wants to be successful. People spend a lot of time and energy pursuing a high quality of life. These are not bad desires. But what *kind* of success is truly worthy of you? What is it that gives life its *highest* quality?

In order to make sure that we don't waste a lot of time and energy on things that don't matter in the end, we should look for the very *best* definition of success and quality of life. That is the focus of this chapter.

DEFINING SUCCESS

Why is the definition of success so important? The answer is that there are different kinds of success, and each person will choose one as the most important. They can all serve a good purpose, but if we focus on views of success that emphasize Level 1 or Level 2 goals and we don't reach those goals, we run the risk of believing that our lives are a waste and a failure.

For example, George thinks that the greatest success in life would be winning a NASCAR race. His goals are to raise enough money to build and maintain a fleet of cars, find a great coach, and win the race. If George spends five years working toward his goals, but then totals his car and injures himself in his very first race, he might think the last five years of his life were a complete waste. If he works hard to raise money again and increases his practice schedule, but then places dead last five years in a row, he would probably think that his entire life was a failure and a waste.

In order to avoid George's dilemma, it is important that we have a definition of success that is worthy of us as human beings. If being successful simply means "winning a car race," then Mother Teresa would have wasted her life, Mahatma Gandhi was a total loser, Martin Luther King Jr. was a big failure, and Jesus would have been better off if He had just stayed home.

The way you choose to define "success" *is very important.*

Whether or not we are conscious of it, each of us carries a definition of "success" in our minds. We do it without even thinking about it. Most people don't sit down and write, "This is what success means for me...." But deep in our hearts, every one of us will form an opinion on what success means.

Sometimes people say or think things like: "I'm a complete failure." Or on the other side: "I've really accomplished what I wanted to do with my life." You probably have a sense of when you are a success and when you are a failure. Most of us get this sense from the expectations of our parents, the opinions of our friends, or signals given to us by teachers, coaches, pastors, or other people whom we respect. We are influenced by what we pick up from the media, television, movies, books, music, social media, and advertising.

Sometimes the expectations that other people have are not at all healthy. They can be incomplete, shortsighted, and even harmful. Have you ever had a coach who cared only about winning, and he drove you so hard that you could just tell it was all he ever thought about? A person like that becomes so obsessed with one single idea of success that you begin to question his mental health. Deep inside you know there's more to life than winning a sports game.

Usually, people who have incomplete, shortsighted, and harmful definitions of success aren't bad people. It's just that *they* are trying to live up to misguided expectations that *they* received from parents, teachers, coaches, and friends when *they* were younger.

But do you really want to spend the rest of your life living up to other people's expectations of success? Why

achievement

goal

God's perspective

momentum

quality of life

self-worth

success

© Alexey Ivanov / iStockphoto

not spend some time thinking about what *you* believe "success" means?

Most people do not spend time thinking about whether their definition of success is truly worthy of them. They default to what contemporary culture tells them will make them successful. What do *you* really think will make your life successful?

The more you reflect on this, the more you may begin to realize that "success" isn't about what you *get*; it's about what you *give*.

"Success" means "achieving a goal." But which goals will lead to a successful life? Suppose you make it to the ripe old age of 90. Looking back at your life, you wonder whether or not you were "successful." Which of your goals will you likely conclude gave your life meaning?

The word success means "achieving a goal."

Just as there are four different ways to view happiness, there are four different ways we can view success. They are all important and they all have a place in our lives. But we will each choose one of these levels of success as the most important—the one we are living for, and the one we think will lead us to a "life well-lived." Let's take a look at the four levels of success, how each one is important, and what happens when we turn each one into our ultimate goal in life.

"SUCCESS" ISN'T ABOUT WHAT YOU GET. IT'S ABOUT WHAT YOU GIVE.

SUCCESS 1

Recall that the first level of happiness comes from physical pleasure and possessions. In this case, the first level of success would mean actually having many possessions, experiencing many pleasures, and never having to experience pain or loss. If that is one's definition of success, then as long as one is achieving it, one will *feel* successful.

So, for example, imagine that you are a Level 1 young adult. Right out of college, you land a great job with a six-figure paycheck, the signing bonus allows you to buy your dream car, and you lay money down on the best condo in town. You're probably thinking, "I've got it made." Translation: *I am a success.*

The way we define happiness is like an engine driving the way we define success. The more we think happiness is about pleasure and possessions, the more we will try to achieve those things. And the more we achieve those things (success), the more we will believe that we are happy.

This creates a kind of *momentum*. **Momentum** means that once the wheel gets rolling, it keeps going by itself. We enjoy money and possessions—they make us feel successful—we're happy. We're happy, and so we seek more money and possessions in order to be more successful. Of course, the major problem with this circular thinking is that we will completely overlook all the other powers, talents, experiences, gifts, and future achievements that we could have. We will be radically *under-living* our lives. The momentum that builds between Happiness 1 and

Success 1 will blind us to other possibilities for even greater happiness.

You may ask, "So what? Why is this a bad thing? As long as I'm happy, who cares about the higher levels?" The problem is not with Level 1 itself, but rather with living *only* for Happiness 1. For most people, doing so will ultimately lead to a *crisis:* boredom, loneliness, emptiness, lack of direction, feelings that we are living beneath ourselves, and low self-esteem. Even worse, the Level 1 crisis can lead to anxiety, depression, substance abuse, and a lower overall sense of well-being.

There are many adults who are stuck on the treadmill of Level 1 success, and who are profoundly unhappy because of it. Take a moment to think of anyone you may know in your own life who seems to be suffering from this.

What will break this cycle?

Rather than wait for the emptiness of Crisis 1 to wake us up and motivate us to escape this trap, it would be better to avoid it from the beginning. We can do this by looking beyond Level 1. Each one of us has the potential to achieve so much more than pleasures and possessions. Each one of us has creativity, talent, skills, intelligence, and many other gifts that can lead to deeper purpose and passion in life.

I think I'm happy.

I try to achieve pleasure and possessions.

I BELIEVE REAL HAPPINESS IS ABOUT PLEASURE AND POSSESSIONS

I get pleasure and possessions.

SUCCESS 2

Success 2 is based on a Happiness 2 point of view. Recall that Happiness 2 comes from winning or being better than others, developing a skill or talent, having power or control, and being popular or admired. So if a person is fixated on Level 2, she will think that she is successful when she is better than other people, has more accomplishments than others, is more popular and more admired than others, etc. These things ground her definition of success.

Most people who turn Level 2 into their idea of true success don't recognize that they are doing this. If asked, they wouldn't tell you that the *only* thing that matters is winning and being better than others. However, when people choose Level 2 as their highest view of happiness, they will subconsciously fall into Success 2.

This often happens because of other people's expectations that reinforce the belief that success means winning and being better than others. If enough people keep telling us this for a long enough period of time, and if we don't spend any time reflecting on whether or not it's true, we will very likely believe it and live our lives accordingly.

So again you might ask: "What's the problem? Why should we care?" The answer is, we should care because everyone wants to be happy. If we live for Level 2 as our highest goal, it can lead to jealousy, fear of failure, aggression, ego-sensitivity, blame, rage, self-pity, feelings of inferiority, feelings of superiority, suspicion, bitterness, contempt, resentment, loneliness, and emptiness. Most people would agree that these feelings do not describe happiness.

We could wait until Crisis 2 overwhelms us and makes us so miserable that we're forced to reconsider what we think success means. In fact, a lot of older people find themselves at this point. But waiting for that to happen causes so much pain, so much time and talent wasted, and so many broken relationships, that perhaps we'd be better off dealing with it now by taking some time for reflection.

As human beings, each one of us has the power for love, generosity, commitment, compassion, empathy, justice, goodness, and self-sacrifice. These powers suggest that we can look beyond Level 2 for a more enduring form of happiness and a more worthy definition of "success."

© pressmaster / Fotolia

SUCCESS 3

Recall from Chapter 1 that Happiness Level 3 comes from doing a good beyond ourselves, being with others, and having empathy for others. Success 3 occurs when something we're doing to achieve a Level 3 goal has a positive outcome.

Consider what happened during a high school varsity football game in Washington state in 2010. With only 10 seconds left in the game, the Snohomish Panthers were losing 35-0 against their longtime rival, the Lake Stevens Vikings.

The losing Panthers had the ball, and their coach wanted Ike Ditzenberger, a team member with Down Syndrome and Type 1 diabetes, to have a chance to carry the ball. So the Panthers coach walked over to the Vikings and said, "I don't want you guys to lose your shutout. You've earned it. But I'd like you to let Ike run around for 10 or 20 yards before you tackle him."

The Vikings agreed, and the play began. Ike took the ball and began to run—first 10 yards, then 20. But the Vikings didn't stop him. Instead, they lunged at him with fake tackle attempts, and let Ike keep going: 30... 40 yards. Ike's teammates played along with fake blocks and the Vikings continued their "barely-miss" dives. The entire student body went nuts and cheered Ike on to a 51-yard touchdown.

Later, the Vikings coach was quoted in the *Seattle Times* newspaper: "This was one of our biggest rivals and we had a chance to shut them out on their home turf. But our players didn't even want to think about that. Their only thought was, 'Let's do the right thing.'" **C**

The rush of Success 3 is different from the feelings that come from Success 2. Both teams felt a connection with Ike, and enjoyed the powerful high of knowing that another human being was happier because they all sacrificed a little of their own egos.

LIVING FOR SUCCESS 3 TAKES WORK AND COMMITMENT.

Once we reach the third level of success, it becomes even more important to do some reflection. Living for Level 3 takes work and commitment. For most of us, it isn't natural to think about the needs of others first. We must let go of many personal desires and comforts in order to make room in our hearts for other people. Thinking about who these people are will help us to avoid the natural tendency to put ourselves first.

Although Level 3 is rewarding, it has a weakness. Recall that the desire for Happiness 3 will eventually become a desire for *perfect* love, *perfect* truth, *perfect* justice, *perfect* beauty, and *perfect* unity. In Level 3, one may begin to think that being successful means being a hero and solving everyone's problems. Unfortunately, because the world is not perfect (and neither are we), one will eventually become frustrated and disappointed.

Consider the story of Joel and his good friend, Iliana, who is devastated that her grandmother has just died. Joel is focused on Level 3 and wants to ease his friend's sadness, so he tells Iliana that everything will be okay. "Don't worry, your Grandma's fine.

Use code **PCS122** to watch Ike's winning touchdown; and code **PCS123** to see Ike receive the 2010 Seattle Children's Inspirational Youth Award.

© Aldo Murillo / iStockphoto

She's in heaven. And you've still got your Grandpa. Look, I'll take you out to a movie and for some ice cream. You'll feel better then." But the more he tries to talk his friend out of her grief, the more Iliana just shakes her head and cries. Eventually, Joel gets frustrated. "Well, I'm only trying to help," he says. Iliana cries harder, and Joel doesn't know what else to do. He feels useless, so he gives up and walks away.

Why did this happen? Because Joel has exaggerated his ability to be Iliana's hero. It's true that Joel can help. He can be with Iliana, listen to her, and hold her when she cries. He can show compassion for Iliana by attending her grandmother's funeral and even praying with Iliana. Joel can do a lot of good, but he cannot be his friend's total hero and turn all her sadness into joy. Only God can do that.

If Joel keeps trying to be Iliana's hero, soon his frustration will destroy his Level 3 virtues. He will no longer be gentle, humble, and loving. He will become too serious, too self-focused, and obsessed with making Iliana happy. Ironically, this may even cause Joel to fall back into a form of Level 2 behavior, where he thinks to himself, "I have to solve Iliana's problem." Do you see the problem with what he has done? Suddenly, success is no longer, "Joel **helping** others." Success has now become "**JOEL** helping others," and it will lead to all kinds of negative emotions like frustration, anger, bitterness, and even despair.

Joel probably didn't intend for things to turn out this way. He really, truly was trying to help. But if you're a Level 3 person and you don't ever stop to think about what success really means, chances are you will make the mistake of trying to be God for everyone without even realizing it.

Fortunately, there is a way to avoid Joel's mistake. God rises above human failures and offers hope and resurrection in the midst of all human tragedies and sadness.

> # GOD RISES ABOVE HUMAN FAILURES AND OFFERS RESURRECTION.

YOUR FREEDOM

As you read the following section, remember that no one can force you to believe in or live out a certain view of success. You have the freedom to choose what you will believe about true success in life. Your freedom is very valuable. The purpose of this section is not to force, it is to propose. It will lay out another view of success which includes God. We include it because it is a very real kind of success experienced by millions of people. We propose it because we think it will lead to greater purpose in your life. But ultimately, the choice is yours. You should understand this level, examine it, and consider its validity very carefully.

SUCCESS 4

Happiness Level 4 comes from surrendering to God's love through prayer, and allowing Him to come to us and help us. Success 4 is what we might call "God's perspective." When God looks at your life, will He think you are a success or a failure? To answer that, we must further ask, how would God define a "successful life?" Obviously, God will not think you are a loser for not making the varsity basketball team. He will not think that you are a failure because you failed a class. He will not think you are useless because you could not solve all your friends' problems.

> **Success 4 is what we might call "God's perspective."**

Have you ever known someone who had a serious illness or injury, and you loved that person very much, but you knew that there was nothing you could do to make him or her get better? Do you remember how this felt? Did you feel helpless, hopeless, desperate, useless, and maybe even angry? Maybe you felt like you failed the person you loved.

It is precisely in situations like this where understanding Success 4 can help. From a Success 4 perspective, not being able to make the person better does not make you a failure. Success 4 occurs when we let go of our desire to be the hero in someone else's life and let God take that role. A person who believes in Success 4 believes that God can and will save the people we love. But from God's perspective, "saving" people is not just about making them live a long time, or preventing everyone from getting injured or ill. His highest goal for us is to help us reach our highest potential—love.

From God's perspective, this life is a tiny part of our overall existence. If that's true, then the more we let go of our own desire to be heroes and let God take that place, the more we will transform our view of success into something deep and lasting.

"Level 4 success" means surrendering to God. From this perspective, the person with the most successful life is the one who has surrendered everything to God. That doesn't necessarily

Dolores Hart was a famous Hollywood movie star from 1947 to 1963. In 1964, the 25-year-old actress gave up everything and became a Roman Catholic nun at the Benedictine Abbey of Regina Laudis in Bethlehem, Connecticut. Many years later, she said, "The fact is, there is a promise given in a [call to the religious life] that is beyond anything in your wildest dreams. There's a gift the Lord offers, and he is a gentleman." In your opinion, did Dolores become more successful or less successful when she left her acting career? Read more about this true story with code **PCS127**.

mean giving away everything you own to charity. It means looking for the ways that God could be using you and the things you own to help others. It means always seeking to love God and our neighbors, no matter where it leads—even if it leads us to places where we don't want to go, such as the bedside of a dying friend or family member.

If we accept and trust God's perspective and let Him occupy the center of our lives, success will come—on God's terms and in God's timing. God's terms are always much better, far more loving, and much longer lasting than our own terms.

One positive outcome of Success 4 is how it helps us pursue Level 3 goals. For example, keeping God in the middle of our lives allows us to more easily rejoice in the successes of other people. When someone is enjoying a video game and won't give up the controls to let you have a turn, instead of getting angry and trying to take the controls away, you might just shake your head, laugh, and enjoy the fact that she's having so much fun. Or when the other team wins a sporting game, you'll be sincere in congratulating them. This doesn't mean you share in their victory, but it does mean that you don't hate them for winning— because you know that in the end, what really matters is God's love for all of you.

GOD'S TERMS ARE MUCH BETTER THAN OUR OWN TERMS.

A second positive outcome of Success 4 is how it helps us to be humble about the good things we've done. This is different from a Level 2 perspective, which thinks, "Thank you, God, for making me so great that I did ten good things compared to Joe's measly two good things." In Level 4 the thought becomes, "Thank you, God, for using me as your tool to get good things done in the world. I like being your partner and letting you be in charge."

A third positive outcome of Success 4 is that there aren't any permanent failures. When seen through God's eternal perspective, He has the time and the power to turn every failure into a success. He can turn evil to good and death to life. Therefore, we don't have to despair when we experience failure—even what might seem to be an ultimate failure. We can say, "Lord, I did my best. Please don't waste the good that I was trying to do. I know you can eventually bring success out of my failure. I trust you, Lord. From now on, if you want my efforts to be successful, then please bless them. And if you don't, then it must mean that you see something bad that will come out of my efforts, so go ahead and make my project fail. I can accept that." There's great freedom in this view of success.

© Michael Chamberlin / Fotolia

If you are interested in learning more about Success 4, or want some tips on how to work on changing your perspective to Success 4, enter code **PCS124**.

DEFINING QUALITY OF LIFE

When was the last time you judged yourself? If you're thinking, "Last week" or "A year ago," you're probably wrong. Human beings judge themselves all the time throughout each day. Sometimes we think things like, "I totally messed up," "My life stinks," or "I wish I could sink through the floor." At other times we might think, "I am a smart person," "I can do this," or "I am so cool."

Sometimes we judge ourselves positively and feel good about ourselves. Have you ever noticed that when you feel good about yourself, it empowers you to do even more? You have more energy, more creativity, and a more positive outlook on life.

But sometimes we judge ourselves negatively. When you feel bad about yourself, it tends to have a bad effect. It drains you of energy, saps your creativity, and can cause you to have a negative outlook on life in general.

For example, Sarah may be doing well in school, and she may have a decent relationship with her mom and dad, but she missed the ball during a volleyball tournament and her team lost because of her. At this particular moment, she feels rotten – like a loser with zero self-worth. Sarah is making a judgment about her "quality of life."

"Quality of life" means how we judge the worth of our lives. Notice in the story above that Sarah's view of her personal worth can change several times a day. These changes often depend on how she happens to be viewing "happiness" and "success" at that moment. This link will become clearer in the next sections.

Quality of life means how we judge the worth of our lives.

List saints or other heroes who used their Level 1 accumulations to make a positive difference to others.

_____

_____

_____

_____

_____

_____

_____

_____

_____

_____

_____

_____

_____

_____

_____

_____

_____

_____

_____

_____

_____

_____

QUALITY OF LIFE 1

People who are primarily focused on Happiness 1, where the goal is to acquire physical possessions and experience pleasure, will tend to judge themselves by what they have and how much they are able to enjoy it. So, for example, Jade has a lot of money and can buy whatever she wants, whenever she wants it. If she is stuck on Happiness 1, then Jade will believe she has a high quality of life _because_ she is rich.

It is true that Jade _does_ have a high Level 1 quality of life. There's nothing wrong with that in itself. Many good people have a high Level 1 quality of life. Some of the greatest saints were wealthy, but they weren't stuck in a Level 1 way of thinking. Since Jade is stuck in Level 1, she will consider _only_ money, material possessions, and physical pleasure when she is judging the worth of her life—her _quality_ of life.

The first problem with Jade's Level 1 fixation is that, in order to continue improving her quality of life, she spends all of her time thinking about how she can acquire more things. In doing so, she will completely miss out on more positive and worthwhile goals, like making a difference in the world and nurturing her faith.

The second problem is that Jade will overlook some very valuable aspects of her nature that are not physical. She will not value her ability to love, her personal skills and talents, her creativity, her sense of humor, and other similar characteristics, unless they help her to accumulate more wealth.

The third problem is this: What happens if Jade loses all of her money, or becomes so sick or old that she can no longer enjoy her possessions? Recall that, because Jade is viewing the world through Level 1, she is judging _herself_ on this level, and has reduced her entire life's purpose to what she has or what she can acquire. When she loses the ability to enjoy these things, she will suddenly believe that her life no longer has meaning or purpose.

You may think, "Well, when that happens, Jade can just switch to Happiness Level 3 and 4, and then she'll be okay." That would be a great solution. But if Jade has spent her entire life living on Level 1, she will find change to be extremely difficult when she is older. She has formed habits and ways of thinking that will be difficult to break. That's why it is so important for us to spend time thinking about these things now.

The fourth problem is that Jade will value other people the same way she values herself; so she will judge other people according to what they have. She won't believe that other people's lives can be worth something simply because they are loving, good, honest, fair, kind, generous, or compassionate, or because of their faith in a loving God. She will not see that another person's life has value simply because he is loved by God. She will judge the worth of other people _only_ by looking at the material things they possess.

Examine how Jade would view the quality of life of the following people:

The elderly. Jade would think that people who are young, independent and healthy have a high quality of life, and people who are old, frail, and not as healthy have a low quality of life. Never mind the fact that older people can frequently have gifts such as wisdom, love, faith, generosity, gentleness, and patience. Jade will not see those things as important. Elderly people cannot move very fast and they get tired a lot. Yes, some of them may have a lot of money, but what's the point when they can't really enjoy it anymore because of their aches, pains, and bad eyesight? How can they enjoy good food without any teeth? Who would want to live like that?

People with disabilities. If they cannot drive a car, walk around, or grasp things in their hands, they would be terribly limited. If they cannot hear or see, they would really be missing out on things like music and video games. And how could they make a lot of money if they have a developmental disability and don't have a high IQ? What's the point of living like that?

Homeless and poor people. Jade would likely wonder—how can people who are homeless and poor have a high quality of life when they don't have nice clothes, cool electronics, and money? She would probably look with contempt at people who are homeless. After all, she is worth more than they are because she has a place to live and they don't. She will look down on families who live in developing countries and have to share a single room together. But is Jade getting something wrong here? Does our quality of life really depend on how many rooms we live in?

© thefinalmiracle / iStockphoto

If you believe that Jade has a very shallow perspective, that's good news. It probably means you are not a Level 1 person. You may have been reading this and thinking, "Hey, wait a minute. My grandmother doesn't have a low quality of life just because she's old," or "I know someone with a disability who seems to be enjoying life," or "I sure don't think I'm worth more than people who have less money than I do." You've probably had enough life experiences to notice that physical pleasure and material things don't buy happiness. It seems neither rational nor responsible to judge the quality of *anybody's* life based on physical pleasure and material things.

Moving beyond a Level 1 view does not mean that we shouldn't work hard to improve Level 1 quality of life for disadvantaged people. But it does mean that we shouldn't judge the value of a person's life by the value of the material things he or she has.

QUALITY OF LIFE 2

In Level 2, where the focus is all on being better than other people, Eddie judges himself by how he compares to everybody else. He will think that he has a really high quality of life if he has achieved more than other people, is more popular than other people, is stronger and more powerful than others, and if others view him as a winner.

These things will become so important to Eddie that he won't even see things like his ability to love, to be generous, and to be kind. Nor will he value these qualities in others. He simply won't care. Similar to people stuck on Level 1, Eddie will probably live only a small part of his life's potential. His life will not be focused on being creative, offering acts of love, having faith, inspiring others, making a difference in the world, or contributing to something good. Instead, Eddie's life will be about *Eddie*, and making sure that other people think he is great. That is how he will judge the quality of his life.

In fact, that is how Eddie will judge the quality of any human life. Elderly people, who cannot compete as well or remember as much as he can, are worth less, in his opinion. People who are poor or homeless and don't wear clothes that are as nice as his are worth less. Physically disabled people who cannot compete athletically, and mentally disabled people who cannot perform academically are worth less to society than people who can compete and who can perform.

IS OUR CULTURE STUCK ON POWER AND ACHIEVEMENT?

The problem with viewing quality of life in terms of Level 2 is that we will see people who are weak and vulnerable in very negative ways. In this view, the more a person loses his ability for Level 2 achievement, the more he not only loses his self-worth, but he also loses "himself." In other words, we will start to think that the person is a "negative." In fact, we can start thinking that these people are somehow less human, or not human at all.

This is not an exaggeration. If an entire culture is stuck on Level 2—focusing only on achievements, power, admiration, and being stronger and better than others—it will affect the way the people in that culture view quality of life, and that in turn, will affect the way they view human beings.

One example of this was in Nazi Germany, where the ideals of power, achievement, and superiority over others became so strong and so rooted in people's thinking that it soon became easy for politically powerful people to use propaganda in order to cause average citizens to view weaker populations as "subhuman."

People who had mental illnesses, learning disabilities, physical deformities, epilepsy, blindness, deafness, and severe alcoholism were called "unfit," "useless eaters," and "life unworthy of life." As many as a quarter of a million of these people were murdered along with Jews and others in the Holocaust because the culture they lived in defined quality of life by Levels 1 and 2.

© Rauluminate / iStockphoto   © Jaren Wicklund / Fotolia

QUALITY OF LIFE 3

In Happiness 3, we start to look at quality of life in a much broader way. Level 3 people believe that life has value because we can make positive contributions to the world which don't necessarily have anything to do with how smart we are, how many athletic abilities we have, or how politically powerful we might be. People can contribute to the world through their ability to be loving, generous, fair, good, sympathetic, truthful, honest, courageous, kind, and peacemakers. People can make a difference through forgiveness, gentleness, and humility. Level 3 people will judge the value of human life based on their ability to live out these qualities.

Think about older people you know and love, such as a grandparent, a neighbor, or one of your parents' older friends. Why do you love these people? Usually, it is not because they are very fast runners, or because they are rich and famous, or powerful. Usually, you love them because they are gentle, patient, kind, humble, honest, fair, generous, wise, and good.

Many people develop these Level 3 traits as they grow older. Obviously, this is not always true (there are plenty of old grouches in the world), but Level 3 often becomes more important to people when they get older because Level 1 and 2 are more difficult to achieve, and because they find that Level 1 and 2 goals are not nearly as satisfying as they once thought.

Take Alan, for example. He is 85, and can't move as fast as he used to. He can't think as clearly as he did when he was younger. He loves playing the oboe in his spare time, but he notices it's getting harder and harder with his arthritis. Yet as Alan slows down, he finds himself becoming gentler, more patient, more understanding of other people's problems, and more interested in helping them.

If Alan were living on Level 1 or 2, he would see aging as a decline in power. He is slowly losing his athletic, academic, and intellectual powers. But if Alan is living on Level 3, he actually sees aging as an increase in powers, such as the power to love, to be gentle, to be humble, etc. In the end, Alan's greater ability for humble love can do more good for the next generation than if he spent years becoming the best oboe player in the world.

© mangostock / Fotolia

If we dismiss elderly people as some cultures have done because we consider them to be "useless eaters," we will dismiss some of the most valuable gifts our culture needs. This is also true of the way we see and treat the poor, the disadvantaged, the weak, and the disabled.

Have you ever wanted to go on a mission trip—say, to build a house for a homeless family in Haiti? Why would you want to go? Is it because you are hoping that the Haitian people will think you are powerful, important, and trendy in your new basketball shoes? Or is it because you think it would be an incredible experience to build a house for someone who doesn't have one? Most likely, it's the second reason. This should tell you something about yourself – that you don't really believe the value or quality of human life is dependent on how we function and perform. It has to do with our hearts.

There is certainly a value to the contributions people make in sports, politics, academics, the arts, business, medicine, and science. But these contributions do not reflect the total value of these peoples' lives. The greatest athlete in the world who can "move mountains but does not have love" (1 Corinthians 13:2) is not pursuing what truly makes life worth living, and is missing out on authentic quality of life.

There is, however, a problem with judging the quality of life *only* by Level 3. A person might start measuring her self-worth through the loving acts that **she** does. This means that it could be easy for her to slip back into a Level 2 mentality and think, "I did a lot of good on that mission trip to Haiti. I helped fifteen people move into a new house. I am a very generous person. Joe over there only helped six people. He is not as generous as I am." If we see the value of our lives *only* through the good acts that we do, we can very easily take ownership of those acts and then slip into a kind of arrogance that is more Level 2 than Level 3. This is why we need Level 4.

QUALITY OF LIFE 4

It should be clear by now that in Happiness 4, a person's focus is on the unconditional love of God; but what does this mean?

God does not place a single condition on His love for us. He does not say "I will love you only if you are rich (Level 1), or if you get an 'A' on your test (Level 2), or if you go to Haiti and build houses for poor people (Level 3)." God's love for us does not depend on **anything** that we **do**. God loves us simply because we **are** who we **are**.

> **Unconditional** = complete or guaranteed, with no conditions, limitations, or strings attached.

This fact—God's unconditional love for us—should completely change the way we judge our value and the value of others. Human value isn't about what we possess, it isn't about what we can do, and it isn't even about how much good we have contributed to the world. We are valuable because God loves us. He loves us just as much when we are evil as when we are good. God loves us all the time. Scripture teaches that He loved us even before we were born. "Before I formed you in the womb, I *knew you*, before you were born I dedicated you" (Jeremiah 1:5). If you look up this passage in the Bible, there may be a footnote which explains that the phrase "knew you" means that God loved us, chose us, and set each one of us apart for Himself before we were even born.

What does this have to do with quality of life? It means that if we are living in Level 4, we understand that the worth of every human being's life is always based on only one measure: that God loves each one of us. Therefore, if we embrace Level 4, we judge our own lives to be unconditionally valuable. There are no limits or tests that one must pass, and nothing that one must prove. Human life is unconditionally valuable because we are loved and desired by God.

If this is true, then every single human person is loved unconditionally by God. *All* people. The homeless. The poor. The destitute. The hungry. The disabled. The elderly. The terminally ill. The weak. The unborn. Those who are social outcasts. Those who are in prison or on death row.

When we achieve Success 4 and see our lives as God does, we rejoice in the insight that our life's quality or value is not dependent on *having* anything, *achieving* anything, or even *doing* anything. Each life has equal quality and value simply because God willed us, created us, and desires us.

GOD LOVES US SIMPLY BECAUSE WE ARE WHO WE ARE.

Although God's love is unconditional, He has given us the ultimate freedom to accept or reject His love. If we are to enter into Quality of Life 4 and experience the joy that comes with it, we have to accept His love. There are three ways to move toward that acceptance.

The first way is to work on overcoming the "seven deadly sins." These sins are pride, greed, lust, envy, gluttony, anger, and sloth. They are also sometimes called the seven "capital"

Use code **PCS126** to access vocabulary and other study tools for this chapter.

sins, because they lead to other sins and vices.

The second way to move toward acceptance of God's love is to build up the kingdom of God as much as you can by leading people to their ultimate dignity and sharing hope with them.

The third way is to build up your own relationship with God in prayer. Our prayer should ask that He inspire and guide us, and that He protect and help us, and it should give thanks to Him for the life that He has given to us.

Three Ways to Move Toward Level 4 Quality of Life

1] Overcome the seven deadly sins.

2] Build up the kingdom of God.

3] Build up your own relationship with God through prayer.

Your teacher, pastor, or school chaplain can help direct you in moving through these steps.

You may be wondering, "If God is going to love us whether we accept His love or not, and whether we work on these three things or not, why should I bother?"

The answer is *not* because we are trying to earn God's love. Rather, it is because Level 4 joy requires a relationship. We cannot receive joy from a love that we refuse to embrace. If we do not do the difficult work of accepting and imitating God's love, we invite the pride, ego, fear, and despair that prevents us from accepting Him.

Secondly, we should work on these three things because they will make us happier. Actively pursuing a Level 4 life will keep us focused on what is truly important.

In short, these three ways to move toward Level 4 quality of life are not forced on us by God, and they are certainly not necessary to earn God's love. But they are the road to ultimate happiness. They help us to accept God's love so that we do not risk rejecting Him, which would lead to under-living our lives, and could lead to our ultimate rejection of Him at the end of our lives.

CONCLUSION

Why did this chapter include a discussion of both success and quality of life? The answer is that we tend to judge the value of our lives (quality of life) by whether or not we have achieved what we think is most important (success). So the way we define success has everything to do with how we view quality of life. If we are stuck in Levels 1 and 2, and we think that success means achieving the most pleasures and accomplishments as is possible, then the way we judge our own value will change from day to day. Some days, we will think we have a lot of self-worth, and other days, we will think we are completely worthless.

But if we are aiming for Levels 3 and 4, and we know that success means achieving the greatest good we can do for others and accepting God's unconditional love, then we will judge our value to be unconditional. We will know that we are never worthless. We are worth more than any *thing* in this entire world. We are worth more than an entire flock of sparrows (Luke 12:7).

CHAPTER 3:
Love

© Helder Almeida / Fotolia

CHAPTER THREE
KEY TERMS

agape

commitment

dignity

empathy

eros

exclusive

humility

intimacy

intrinsic dignity

love

philia

storge

In the English language, we use the word "love" when talking about things like our favorite foods, movies, or music. In this chapter we focus on how we use the word when referring to relationships between persons.

If we were to analyze the lyrics of every popular song that made it to a "Top 10" chart over the last decade, the one word we would see more often than any other noun or verb is "love." If it's true that music reveals the deepest desires of the human heart, then love is apparently at the top of the list. Our desire for love is closely related to happiness. Ask anybody, "Why do you want to be loved?" and they will probably answer, "Because love will make me happy."

When was the last time you sat down and asked yourself what love means? This is an extremely important question, because if you don't make up your *own mind* about what love means, you will most likely allow *other people* to define it for you.

There is no shortage of people trying to influence your beliefs—Hollywood and the entertainment industry; advertising and the news media; retailers and the fashion industry; books, magazines, and websites; schools and teachers; even political parties and groups that promote cultural change—they all have messages about what love means. Often these voices give contradictory definitions. They can't all be correct.

Unless we spend time doing some real reflection, there's a good chance we will simply absorb whatever the loudest voice in the culture claims is the "true" definition of love. We risk defending something that, deep inside, we don't really believe. We might even make choices that will not only hurt us, but could make us feel like we are betraying ourselves and working against our own goals for happiness and fulfillment.

You shouldn't have to settle for whatever the popular culture is telling you to believe. Love is too important. Imagine if you were at a fine restaurant and the waiter said, "Oh, you're just a teenager. You don't get the full menu. You only get this one…" and he handed you a children's menu that listed hot dogs and macaroni. You would probably feel insulted. You would know that you weren't being taken seriously as a

If you've ever waited in the checkout line at a grocery store, you've probably seen the magazines and tabloids that focus on the lives of celebrities. You might see a headline about a famous actress who left her fourth husband to find "true love" in yet another relationship. How do you think the editors of such magazines define "love"?

© Ravi Tahilramani / iStockphoto

customer, and you might think, "Hey, wait a minute—why can't I have the *whole* menu?"

Yet this is exactly what many voices in our culture say to teenagers. They assume that young people will *never* act responsibly and cannot understand deeper and more self-sacrificial forms of love. This is especially true in the areas of relationships and sexuality. Many movies, television programs, songs, fashions, and advertisements convey a message that says, "Oh, you're a teenager. You don't understand love and you can't be responsible. You're going to mess up. Just be careful if you have sex, and we grown-ups will fix it later if you get pregnant." That is insulting. Anyone who tells you that is trying to cheapen you.

If you decide that you *prefer* the definition of love offered by the popular culture, you have the freedom to choose it. But you have a right to see the *full* menu of options before deciding to settle for less. Only then can you make a real choice about how you want to live your life.

As you may have guessed, your definition of happiness will have a significant effect on how you define love. People tend to view love through the same lens that they view happiness. Just as there are four levels of happiness, there are four levels of love. The higher levels of love (3 and 4) are deeper, longer lasting, and more fulfilling than the lower levels.

OUR VIEW OF HAPPINESS AFFECTS OUR VIEW OF LOVE.

Throughout this chapter, we will recall the important things you learned in Chapter 1 on happiness. But if you are having trouble with some of the comparisons between love and happiness in this chapter, feel free to go back and review Chapter 1.

FOUR DIFFERENT KINDS OF LOVE

Before we explore the four different LEVELS of love, we need to discuss four different KINDS of love. That can be a little confusing, but think of the *kinds* of love as different *ways* to love somebody. Some ways of loving go much deeper and are more fulfilling than others, and are easier to do if you are a Level 3 or Level 4 person.

From a faith perspective, all of these kinds of love are good. You will see in the upcoming sections how God loves each one of us in *all four* of these different ways. You will also learn why a faith perspective considers the *fourth* kind of love to be the deepest.

STORGE

The ancient Greek philosophers Plato and Aristotle were the first to formally identify different kinds of love nearly 2,400 years ago. Thus, it's no surprise that the four kinds of love have Greek names. The first kind is called *storge* (pronounced *STORE-gay)*. It means a spontaneous feeling of affection or delight toward someone or something. Imagine that you are at the mall and you see a cute 18-month-old child toddling around her mother and giggling. You don't know her, but in a moment of fun she runs up to you, hugs your leg, and grins. You would probably be amused, and feel affection and delight. Similar feelings might be experienced with a close friend who always makes you laugh, or even with a cute pet, like a dog or cat.

There's nothing wrong with this kind of love. *Storge* is good. It certainly plays a part in how God loves us. He has affection for His children, and takes delight in us. But *storge* is not very deep. It doesn't require much from us. Think of the example of the toddler at the mall—it wasn't necessary to have a prior relationship with the child in order to be charmed by her behavior. You might smile or laugh with the child and her parents, but you aren't required to "do anything" or "be anything" in return for having experienced this moment of *storge* love.

PHILIA

The Greeks called the second kind of love *philia* (pronounced *FEE-lee-uh)*, which refers to friendship. *Philia* love is characterized by two people who share interests and who are willing to "give and take" in their relationship.

As friends, the two people have expectations of each other that make the relationship different from *storge*. For example, if Susan remembers Allison's birthday, she may come to expect that Allison will remember *her* birthday. If birthdays are very important to Susan, but Allison forgets Susan's birthday or doesn't care enough to do anything about it, then Susan may decide she doesn't want to be friends with Allison anymore.

Philia love is good. We should have relationships where we expect things from one another. Certainly God loves us this way. We expect that He will provide for our needs, and He expects that we will trust Him and follow His Word. But *philia* is not the deepest kind of love, because it does not require intimacy. Friendships can be shallow and superficial. They can be short-term. They can get started for a mutually beneficial purpose and then end as soon as that purpose has been fulfilled.

For example, suppose you are on vacation at the beach with your family and you join in a game of volleyball with some other teenagers you just met. You have a great time and spend the next two mornings playing volleyball with them. But then your vacation ends, you go back home, and you never see your beach friends again. That doesn't mean the friendship wasn't valuable, but it wasn't very deep. The length and level of commitment or contribution that is required in a *philia* friendship can vary a great deal.

EROS

The third kind of love is *eros* (pronounced *EAR-oss).* This includes romantic love, or a love that is characterized by deep intimacy. An example would be a husband and wife who love each other intimately, exclusively, and sexually. They have a deep commitment to one another.

Just like the other kinds of love, *eros* is good. God loves us intimately, and has made a deep commitment to each of us. In fact, He loves you so intimately that it can feel as though He loves you *exclusively*—as if you were the *only* person on earth that He loved.

Still, *eros* is not the deepest kind of love. For example, a husband and wife do not feel intimately close to each other all the time. There can be times when they feel a bit disconnected as the busy nature of life gets in the way. *Eros* is also not the kind of love that motivates a person to go on a mission trip to help serve the poor in the Philippines. That requires a deeper kind of love.

AGAPE

Agape is the fourth kind of love (pronounced *uh-GA-pay*). This is *selfless* love that is characterized by having a humble and gentle heart, and by forgiveness, mercy, peacemaking, generosity, patience, kindness, and compassion. It comes from recognizing that all human beings are unique and precious, and precisely because of those qualities, human beings are worthy of *our* love and the love of *others* as well.

Agape means making a difference beyond ourselves to something bigger, and wanting what is actually and really good for others. *Agape* love includes *empathy*, which means being able to feel what someone else is feeling, and understand what someone may be going through. *Agape* can be defined as having so much empathy for someone else that you want to become a part of his life in order to do good for him and help to make his life better. You have so much empathy for this other person that you form a bond with him in your heart so that doing what is good for him becomes just as easy, if not easier, than doing what is good for yourself.

Empathy means being able to feel what someone else is feeling.

Consider the example of a student named Brad on the next page.

Four Types of Love

Storge	AFFECTIONATE LOVE	*Storge* means a spontaneous feeling of affection or delight toward someone or something.	affection
Philia	FRIENDSHIP LOVE	*Philia* means a friendship love that involves give and take.	same interests, mutual commitment
Eros	ROMANTIC LOVE	*Eros* is a romantic love characterized by deep intimacy and commitment.	intimate, exclusive, sexual
Agape	SELFLESS LOVE	*Agape* is a selfless love that recognizes the unique preciousness of each and every other human being.	humble, gentle, generous, forgiving, compassionate, etc.

Brad is enrolled in a biology class. On the first day of class, the teacher assigns each student a lab partner to work with throughout the semester. Brad doesn't care much for his assigned partner, a classmate named Viktor. Their personalities are very different, and so are their work habits. Viktor and his parents are immigrants from Russia, so Viktor has an accent that Brad finds difficult to understand. Brad enjoys cracking jokes, but Viktor never laughs, probably because his cultural background makes it hard for him to "get" the humor. On a good day Brad finds Viktor to be an incredible bore, and on bad days he finds him downright irritating.

One Monday morning Brad shows up to class and his teacher pulls him aside. He tells Brad that he will be assigned a new lab partner because Viktor has been pulled out of the class for the rest of the semester. When Brad asks why, his teacher informs him that Viktor's father was killed over the weekend in an automobile accident.

Brad is shocked. Throughout class all he can think about is how terrible he would feel if his father died like that, suddenly and unexpectedly. He thinks about Viktor's grief and feels it intensely in his own heart. He wonders about Viktor's family, how his mother must feel, and whether Viktor has brothers or sisters who are also sharing in this trauma. Suddenly, instead of seeing Viktor as just a "problem" or an annoying person that he'd rather not deal with, Brad thinks of him as another human being who has the same feelings and the same vulnerabilities that he has.

Brad makes an effort to find Viktor's address and phone number. He feels moved to send him a sympathy card. Then he finds the courage to call Viktor on the phone. It is an awkward conversation, since the two don't have much in common. Yet Brad can tell that Viktor is surprised and grateful for this act of compassion.

He learns that Viktor is the oldest of five children, and that his mother is terribly worried about how their family will survive without the father's income. Viktor wants to find a job to help support his family, since he is now the "man of the house." Later on, Brad remembers that his own father, who runs a successful landscaping business, had been talking about hiring some additional laborers because he was having trouble keeping up with work. Brad talks to his dad, and makes arrangements for Viktor to meet him. Viktor is given a good-paying landscaping job in the mornings and on weekends that will allow him to stay in school while earning money to help his family.

Use code **PCS132** to learn more about the four kinds of love online.

In this story, we can see that Brad certainly did not start off feeling any kind of *agape* love for Viktor. But the tragedy in Viktor's life opened Brad's eyes and softened his heart. It inspired him to "get outside of himself" and place the needs of another human being first, above his own needs.

Agape love is very good, and God loves us in this way. In fact, He has so much empathy for us that His only Son entered our world, became one of us, and then offered Himself as a sacrifice to prove His unconditional love.

Agape is the deepest kind of love because it has powers that are not found in the other kinds of love:

1] It allows us to love *all* human beings without exception.

2] It requires sacrifice from us without any expectation of reward.

3] When *agape* love is perfected, we can love and forgive an enemy who hates us, despite the fact that we have no affection (*storge*) for her.

4] We can love and care for a poor family in need, even though we don't expect them to be able to return our act of generosity (*philia*).

5] We can love and have compassion for a dying elderly man even though we don't have any romantic feelings (*eros*) for him.

FOUR LEVELS OF LOVE

Now that we've learned the four different *kinds* of love, we can discuss the four different *levels* of love. These levels relate closely to the four levels of happiness, and we will see which kinds of love can be experienced in each level of love.

LOVE 1

Recall that in Happiness Level 1, we have desires for things that are "external," or outside of ourselves, and these desires involve things that we can see, taste, touch, hear, or smell. Furthermore, we want the **immediate gratification** of these desires. That means we want physical pleasure right away without having to wait—such as ignoring chores and homework in order to run out and grab pizza with some friends who just arrived at the door.

If the primary focus of our lives is to experience Happiness 1, we will think that love is a *feeling* we get from something physical that is outside of us. Bob will love Sue if it *feels good* to be around her. Which of the four *kinds* of love can a Level 1 person experience?

STORGE IN LOVE 1

Love 1 can include *storge* because *storge* is a feeling of affection. A puppy feels affection when you pet it or feed it. A Level 1 person would feel affection for the same reason—because you are giving him something he wants, and making him feel good.

PHILIA IN LOVE 1

Love 1 can include friendships, but they are what Aristotle called "friendships of pleasure," or "friendships of utility." For example, Janet thinks that "friendship" is about somebody making her feel good by giving her things that she wants when she wants them. But in order to make sure that happens, she will have to try to control her friends. She will order them around constantly. She will make many demands, and will have expectations that they will give her things, invite her to social gatherings, and allow her to use their belongings.

Of course, since Level 1 is very self-focused, Janet won't feel that she needs to treat her friends the same way in return. She will try to find friends who give her a lot without asking for much from her in return. If she cannot find that, Janet will try to get away with only giving what she has to, in order to get what she wants. She may hide what she has from others and will even lie about it, just so she can avoid sharing it.

Clearly, Janet will end up using her friends and treating them like they are her "play things." If they don't give in to her demands, Janet will decide they are *not* good friends, and she will dump them and look for new friends.

There are people who act like Janet because they have bad intentions. But there are also people who do this because it is *all they have ever learned,* and they don't know any other way of functioning in a relationship. They may have been in an abusive relationship in which others treated them the same way. This can lead them to fall into a Level 1 pattern of behavior without even realizing it.

If you have a friend who is treating you this way, you deserve better. A person who is using you this way is not a real friend. In order to protect your self-worth, you should talk to that person and ask him or her to start treating you with more dignity and fairness. If the other person will not do this, you might talk to your parents, teacher, pastor, coach, counselor, or some other trusted adult about whether you should continue this friendship. Reflect on how Jesus treated His friends, as told in the Gospels. That is how you deserve to be treated by your friends.

HOW JESUS TREATED HIS FRIENDS IS HOW YOU DESERVE TO BE TREATED BY YOUR FRIENDS.

If you think that YOU might be stuck in Level 1 and are treating people badly, you probably don't feel very good about it. You probably realize that you are missing out on friendships that are deeper and much more rewarding. You also deserve better. You are hurting yourself, and it might be because someone else has hurt you and has led you to believe that manipulating other people to get what you want is the only way to be happy. That isn't true. A trusted adult can help. It is an act of courage to tell someone you are struggling and to ask for help.

_____
_____
_____
_____
_____
_____
_____
_____
_____
_____
_____
_____
_____
_____
_____
_____
_____
_____
_____
_____
_____
_____
_____
_____

EROS IN LOVE 1

Love 1 can also include feelings of romantic love, but that is as far as Love 1 goes—feelings. Consider Ethan, who is a total Level 1 guy. He thinks that "being in love," means "being physically attracted to a pretty girl." He is dating Beth.

Ethan believes that Beth loves him only if she gives him what he wants, and what he wants is a sexual relationship. If she refuses or makes him wait, Ethan will accuse Beth of not really loving him. Just as in a non-romantic friendship, Ethan will have to try to control the person he is in love with. After all, if Beth is totally free of his control, she may not give him what he wants all the time. So Ethan will say and do whatever he thinks will work to pressure Beth to give him the pleasure he wants. And since his perception of romance is all about feeling good, he won't see anything wrong with getting sexual pleasure with other girls any time he wants.

If Beth objects to this behavior, Ethan will either accuse her of not really loving him, or he may abuse, threaten, or dump her. If he wants to keep her around, he may lie about his behavior. These are all ways of controlling Beth, as if she were just a sexual object. Ethan doesn't really care about her as a person. He doesn't care about her future. Furthermore, his own future is at risk from this behavior, though he probably does not recognize this. He only cares about how Beth makes him feel right now.

When Ethan turns Beth into a thing, he acts like she doesn't have any self-worth. If Beth allows Ethan to treat her this way, it will likely damage her own sense of self-worth, assuming she had a sense of self-worth to begin with.

It is impossible to build an intimate relationship in Level 1. Intimacy means to open up the deepest parts of yourself to another person: physically, spiritually, emotionally, and psychologically. Intimacy does not not hide anything, and allows the other person to "see you as you really are." You are not pretending to be something that you are not.

ARE YOU YOUR TRUE SELF? OR PRETENDING TO BE SOMEONE YOU'RE NOT?

If Ethan is treating Beth like a thing, like a sexual object, he will not see any value in opening up the deepest parts of himself to Beth. What would be the point? It takes too much time and effort.

All Ethan wants is to "own" Beth's beauty and to get sexual pleasure from it. If Beth pushes Ethan to open up his heart and soul, he will become annoyed. He may pretend to open up just to make her stop nagging him, but it won't be real intimacy. It's all just an act to get what he wants.

At the same time, Beth will find it impossible to be intimate with Ethan because she knows she can't trust him with her heart and soul. Beth is not dumb. She knows Ethan is just using her for sexual pleasure, and so she holds most of her heart back. If she believes that there is more to their relationship than just Level 1, she may try to give him some of her heart. But in

© Tatyana Gladskih / Fotolia

the end, Ethan will use that too to control her even more and manipulate her into giving him more pleasure. Beth is setting herself up for a broken heart. Ethan doesn't care about that. Owning Beth as a beautiful possession is good enough for him, even if he destroys her sense of dignity and misses out on true intimacy.

When we discuss Love 3 and Love 4 later on, we will see the enormous gift that Ethan is missing out on. But unless he moves to the higher levels of love, he won't see it. That's a real tragedy, because in Love 1, Ethan will never have the generosity and intimacy that are essential for a healthy family life. In the end, no woman will ever be able to please Ethan forever. He will wander from woman to woman, creating a reputation of using and abusing them.

Now, this does *not* mean that healthy romantic love and physical attraction cannot go hand in hand. Most people are drawn toward a romantic relationship because of a spark of physical attraction, and that is not a bad thing. The problem happens when somebody *reduces* a romantic relationship to *only* physical beauty and to the feelings that come out of it. If this happens, the other person in the relationship is reduced to a "thing" or an "object." That other person will probably not appreciate feeling like a thing, and may end the relationship. Or if that person accepts being treated like a thing, he or she will have a squashed sense of dignity, intimacy, and freedom, and will not be in a healthy relationship.

AGAPE IN LOVE 1

People who are stuck in Level 1 usually don't understand the importance of *agape*. *Agape* is about doing what is good for others and caring about the needs of others. But Level 1 only focuses on our own physical needs. If we stay stuck in Level 1, we will never experience the kind of love that allows us to know compassion for others who are in need, or empathy for others who are hurting, or forgiveness for those who have hurt us. Without *agape*, we will never be able to understand God's love for us—which occurs in all of the ways just mentioned.

© fatihhoca / iStockphoto

LOVE 2

Remember that Happiness Level 2 is all about the **ego**. Somebody who is stuck in Level 2 is comparing herself to everybody else, and is thinking only about being more successful, more powerful, and more popular than others.

If someone is primarily seeking Happiness Level 2, she is not going to think that love is about what she can give to others. She will think that love is about being admired by others. Giving love won't be nearly as important to her as being loved. It will be a one-way street. Given these limitations, what kinds of love can a Level 2 person experience?

STORGE IN LOVE 2

People who function on Level 2 can experience *storge* (feelings of affection), because it doesn't require them to sacrifice any of their ego.

PHILIA IN LOVE 2

They can also have friendships of pleasure or utility, and can experience what the Greek philosopher Aristotle called "intellectual friendships." An intellectual friendship is when you become friends with another person because he or she makes you feel smart, important, popular, and even superior to other people.

Unfortunately, friends like this usually reinforce each other's feelings of being superior to everyone else, and they look at those who are not in their group as being inferior. Here is an example:

Zach thinks that his friends ought to admire him. Since life is all about ego-gratification, then a "true friend" will appreciate him, think he's really cool, and boost his self-esteem. A true friend will help Zach feel more powerful, more independent, and more popular. Unfortunately, the closer they get to Zach, the more his friends see his weaknesses. When they point out those weaknesses, Zach will be offended. He may even get angry. Friends have no business challenging his superiority, Zach thinks. This is threatening to him. The very purpose of a friend in Level 2 is to increase his self-esteem, so most of Zach's friendships do not last very long.

Some of Zach's friends begin to notice that they are being used to boost his ego. They don't like it, so they drift away. Others begin to notice some of his weaknesses and point them out, so Zach gets rid of them and looks for other people who will admire his superiority.

There is nothing wrong with wanting people to notice our talents or good qualities. There is nothing wrong with wanting our friends to think we are unique and special. We *are* unique and special. But if we *reduce* friendship to a "fan club," we will end up hiding our true selves and we will resent it any time our friends point out our flaws. Our friendships will be very shallow and superficial. In the long run, people will not like being around us because they will sense that we are using them to boost our own egos.

Often, people end up like Zach because, deep down, they don't believe they are *intrinsically* valuable.

Intrinsically valuable means to be valued for who you are as a human being, and not for anything you have or can do.

This means they do not sense that they are valuable *on the inside.* They do not believe their value comes from the simple fact that they are human and loved by God. They think that what makes them valuable is that they are *better than* other people—more popular, talented, intelligent, and powerful. They tell themselves that no one could possibly like them for who they are on the inside, and so they have to convince people that they are *superior* in order to be *liked.*

The three main problems with Level 2 friendships are:

1] We are *using* people in our circle of friends to satisfy our egos and to make ourselves feel important. Our friends probably know this, and there is a good chance they may be using us as well. Such friendships are not very deep.

2] Because we are using each other, there aren't any true *commitments* in the friendship. People will abandon and even betray one another in order to remain popular or superior.

3] These friendships usually don't last very long because people get bored of telling us how great we are, or they discover our weaknesses. When that happens, we are likely to move on to new, shallow relationships with people who will see only our superior qualities.

EROS IN LOVE 2

Level 2 people can experience *eros*, but similar to Level 1, it is usually a very self-centered kind of romantic love. It focuses on being loved by the other person. Wanting to be loved by the other person isn't wrong—it is a very important part of romantic relationships. But if we don't also have an equal care and concern for the good of the other person, the relationship remains stuck in Level 2 and is very unhealthy. We can see how this works in the story of Marie and Todd.

Marie's life goals are focused on Level 2. She is dating Todd because he is running for a seat in the U.S. Senate. Marie dreams of being married to a United States Senator and going to fancy parties. She looks forward to meeting important people and being respected by her family and friends. Todd thinks that she loves him, but Marie is really in love with the *idea* of being married to a man who would be powerful and admired, and who could make her powerful and admired too.

One day Todd tells Marie that he wants to drop out of the Senate race. The pressure is too much. What he really wants is to go back to his family business, get married, and raise children with Marie. Marie is appalled and feels let down. "How can you do this to me? All you think about is yourself!" she cries, and immediately leaves him. Todd is left feeling confused, rejected, and depressed.

Marie's problem was *not* that she wanted her future husband to do well in life. Romantic love should include a desire for the other to develop his or her skills. Couples should encourage one another to become the best person possible, using whatever gifts God has bestowed. But Marie reduced romantic love to the idea that she would ride with her fiancé to greatness so that *she* could be great. It was not about helping Todd find the plan that God had for him; it was about making sure Todd stuck to the plan *Marie* had for him—a plan that ended with *her* being powerful and admired.

If a couple like Todd and Marie are sexually involved, the situation will have even more harmful consequences. Marie may have used sex to manipulate Todd's heart and make him more committed to her. Todd thought that he was giving himself away to a woman who loved him, and that she was giving herself to him for the same reason, but that would not be true. In fact, Marie was using Todd to advance herself. Once she saw that he was not following her plan and that she could not control him, she abandoned him.

When they were sexually involved, Todd believed that it was more than just *physical* intimacy. He thought that they were also being emotionally and spiritually intimate. But Marie was using her body to tell a lie to Todd. She was deceiving him in order to get what she wanted. When she dumps him, he will feel used and will suffer a great deal. His self-esteem will be hurt and he will find it very difficult to trust any woman in the future. He may begin to doubt that love can ever be real, and conclude that the close intimacy he has always yearned for is just a cruel illusion. He may even view himself as unlovable and unworthy of true emotional and spiritual intimacy.

Since Marie is only thinking about herself, she probably does not realize that the damage she has caused to Todd not only cuts very deeply, but could also last long into his future and could negatively affect many other people in Todd's life.

For her part, Marie will suffer too. She will never really be happy because she can never be intimate. She has to hide her heart and her soul, because her true intentions are selfish and she cannot let the men she dates know this. If she does, she will risk losing a potential mate. So Marie is fake, shallow, and immature in her relationships. She will find herself dating men who are content to have superficial relationships, due to their own problems. Because of this, she is unlikely to have a relationship of deep trust with any man unless she can somehow move herself to a higher level of happiness and develop a deeper view of love.

There are several very important lessons to learn from Marie's story.

If we want to avoid these problems, we have to move from Level 1 and 2 thinking into Level 3 and 4 thinking. As we will see later, the kind of love we experience in Levels 3 and 4 is deeper, much longer lasting, and far more fulfilling than love that uses and abandons people over and over again.

Many people in their teens or twenties are still forming beliefs about what love is. If you are just beginning to discover love, it is important to understand that you have an entire lifetime in front of you—and you deserve a future that is filled with *true* love. If you are a Level 3 or Level 4 person, you should protect yourself and your heart. This includes being cautious about attractions to people who are still stuck in Level 1 or Level 2. Think carefully about the consequences of being in a romantic relationship with someone who does not share your deeper view of happiness, self-worth, and love.

A Level 3 or 4 person can be tempted to think, "How is the Level 1 or 2 person ever going to find true love unless someone like me helps him move to a higher level? I can change him!" That is possible—but it is also extremely unlikely. Even if you manage to change that person, it will require an enormous amount of time, work, pain, heartache, failures, sacrifice, and loneliness on your part.

It is more likely that the Level 1 or Level 2 person will manipulate you and even convince you to give up some or all of your Level 3 or Level 4 beliefs and values, or will end up breaking your heart. That does not mean the person can never change. But *you* may not be the best person to motivate that change. A romantic relationship is usually not the best way to help someone jump a level. That's because there are too many emotions, very different expectations on both sides, and too much close personal involvement to see clearly and understand what the other person really needs.

As trite as it sounds, sometimes really loving someone means letting him or her go.

> # DO YOU CARE ABOUT THE OTHER PERSON EQUALLY? OR DO YOU JUST WANT TO BE LOVED?

AGAPE IN LOVE 2

People who are stuck in Level 2 will usually have an even more difficult time moving to *agape* love than people in Level 1. That doesn't mean that Level 2 people don't care about others and don't want to make a positive difference in the world. They sometimes do. But they are so focused on themselves that two things usually happen.

First, because they are so busy thinking about themselves, the good they are trying to do turns into a comparison game where they look at everyone else and say, "Hey… I'm doing more good than you are," or, "The good that I am doing is more important than what you are doing."

Second, when that happens, their ego and their need to have others recognize them and think that they are great tends to overshadow any good they are trying to do.

To really experience *agape*, we need to move to Love 3 and Love 4.

LOVE 3 CAN BE DEFINED IN THE FOLLOWING WAY:

> "WANTING WHAT IS GOOD FOR THE OTHER SO MUCH THAT IT BECOMES JUST AS EASY, IF NOT EASIER, TO DO THE GOOD FOR THE OTHER AS IT IS TO DO THE GOOD FOR MYSELF."

LOVE 3

Happiness Level 3 is experienced by doing good for others. Let's explore this further.

The first part of Happiness 3 is to **"want what is good for the other."** In Love 3, we recognize the very real worth and goodness inside of every human being, including ourselves. This true worth and goodness is called "intrinsic dignity." We see the deception in thinking that our lives have meaning only because of some *thing* that we own, or because of some *skill* or *talent* that we have. We understand that our existence is good because we are capable of love and goodness. Since we can see that in ourselves, we can also see it in other people. This recognition makes us want to do good for others.

For example, Courtney has a school project in which she has to perform an act of service for some needy person in the community, and then write a report on her experiences. She decides to volunteer for an elderly man who lives down the street by going over in the evenings and washing his dishes every night for four weeks. This elderly man has a grandson named Hayden who comes over on Monday nights to watch football with his grandfather. Hayden is very good looking, and Courtney is attracted to him.

If Courtney's *real* motivation is to be around Hayden in the hopes that he will ask her on a date, she doesn't have Love 3 for her elderly neighbor. She's not really interested in helping him; she's interested in getting a date with his grandson. Courtney may think to herself, "So what? I'm still doing his dishes every night. Isn't that

© Jaren Wicklund / iStockphoto

The characteristics of Love 3 are perfectly described in the Bible in 1 Corinthians 13. Here we learn that love is not selfish. It is not rude or jealous. It includes patience, kindness, forgiveness, empathy, self-sacrifice, care, concern, compassion, gentleness, and humility. Open a Bible and read though this passage slowly. Use the lines on the next few pages of this chapter to write down what you think about each of the characteristics of love.

the point? If I get a date at the same time, what difference should it make to the old man?" The difference is that Love 3 is not simply about doing a good act. It's about forming a unity and a bond with someone, so that he knows you care about him as a human being. Courtney's elderly neighbor is probably perceptive enough to figure out that she is there only to get a good grade in her class, and perhaps to get a date with his grandson. Just because he is elderly does not mean he is no longer human. He may feel sad, lonely, and used by this.

The point of Love 3 is not to use people for our own selfish purposes. The point is to *want* what is good for the other *"for his own sake"* —not so that *we* can be happy, but so that *he* will be happy. Love 3 is generous.

The second part of the definition of Love 3 is to **"do the good"**. So even though Love 3 is not *just* about doing a good act, it should *include* good acts. For example, let's look at a young man named Glenn. He thinks he's a Level 3 guy because he really *wants* good things to happen to people, but he never does anything about it. One day he sees two bullies picking on a smaller child after school. He thinks

to himself, "That's terrible. That poor kid. How can they do that to him?" And he even says a prayer, "Dear Jesus, please help that kid get away from those guys." But Glenn doesn't want to get involved and risk getting hurt, so he crosses over to the other side of the street, looks away, and keeps walking. Glenn is more concerned about himself than the smaller boy.

The third part of the definition of Love 3 is that "**it becomes just as easy, if not easier, to do the good for the other as to do the good for myself.**" At first, it is quite difficult to do good for others before ourselves. It does not come naturally to most of us. We have to learn to put others before ourselves, and then we have to practice it often. Love 3 is difficult work. But if we keep trying, it will become easier and easier until eventually it becomes "second nature" —it becomes a habit. The more natural it becomes to do good for others rather than for ourselves, the more we move into Love 3.

Now let's consider how Level 3 people can experience the four kinds of love.

STORGE IN LOVE 3

Just like people who are oriented toward Levels 1 and 2, people in Level 3 can feel *storge* (affectionate love). But because they are concerned about the needs of others above the needs of themselves, they don't just feel *affection* for others—they feel *responsible* for others.

PHILIA IN LOVE 3

Friendships in Level 3 are much deeper than in Levels 1 and 2. The basis for a friendship in Level 3 is that "we find joy in loving what is lovable." Rather than seeing friendship as a tool to help enhance our self-esteem, we are seeking to do the good for the other for the sake of the other. We recognize the intrinsic worth, dignity, and goodness of the other.

Healthy Level 3 friendships require each person to make some level of *commitment*, which means that we share some time, energy, talents, and other gifts with friends. Keeping a commitment is not just easier when a person has a Level 3 attitude, it is essential. If someone is stuck in Level 1, his commitment to a relationship will end as soon as he realizes that it is no longer making him *feel good*. If he is stuck in Level 2, his commitment will end when he senses that it is no longer useful for *affirming his superiority to others*. But a Level 3 person will keep his commitments to a friend out of respect for the friendship itself.

If both persons in a friendship are on Level 3, it becomes much easier for them to pursue goals and interests that they share in common. This is because their focus is on the other person rather than on fulfilling their own ego needs. Their friendship will not be burdened by a need to feel superior or to control the other.

For example, Nicole, who has studied Spanish for five years, volunteers at her church to help Spanish-speaking children learn English. She is excited about how her skill can be used to make someone's life better. At the training, she is partnered with a girl named Anna who shares Nicole's enthusiasm about making a difference in the lives of others. They become instant friends and are given the assignment of tutoring four children on weekends.

After a few sessions, Nicole discovers that tutoring is hard work and she is disappointed with her progress. The children seem bored and she feels like she's not connecting with them. Meanwhile, Anna is doing fine. Her Spanish is better than Nicole's, and she is very clever at coming up with little games and songs to help the children learn how to say words and phrases in English. Nicole tries using some of Anna's techniques. Much to her surprise, it works! The children start paying attention and begin to learn what she is teaching.

One day after tutoring, the two girls go out to lunch. Nicole tells Anna that she has a real gift and should consider teaching as a career. She thanks Anna for everything she's learned from watching her: "I feel like these children are learning twice as fast because of the tips I've picked up from you." Anna responds by telling Nicole that she has learned a lot about patience and perseverance by watching *her* work with the children, and Nicole is pleasantly surprised to hear this. Anna laughs and says, "We make a good team. Maybe we should learn more languages and start a full-time tutoring business."

In this story, we can see the difference that Level 3 makes in a relationship. When Nicole sees that Anna has talents and skills that she does not have, she chooses to focus on how the *students* are benefiting. Realizing that Anna has a unique gift, she brings it to Anna's attention and encourages her to develop it even further. Why would Nicole do this? Because in Level 3, she *sees* the good in her friend, and *wants* what is good for her, as well as for the many other people whose lives will be helped. When Level 3 people see others using their talents to make the world a better place, they don't feel envy or resentment. Instead they feel *joy*—because their vision is not distorted by their own egos.

It is also important to consider Anna's reaction. When Nicole tells her that she has great talent, Anna doesn't say: "Why yes, thank you for recognizing that I am vastly superior to you in almost every way. Please tell me more about my incredible talents." Instead, Anna's reaction is to return the compliment. Anna wants to affirm the good in Nicole, because she is inspired by her perseverance even when things turned out to be more difficult than Nicole expected.

EROS IN LOVE 3

People in Level 3 can certainly experience romantic love. In fact, a Level 3 focus is essential if we are to "rescue" *eros* from the pitfalls that can happen in Levels 1 and 2. We can see this most clearly when we look at sexual relationships. If a person is stuck in Level 1, he will see sexuality as a quest to aggressively pursue, conquer, and "own" another beautiful person. If he is stuck in Level 2, he will see sexuality as a quest to have someone else affirm his desirability and strengthen his ego.

But in Level 3, sexuality is transformed. Sexuality is now seen as an *intimate gift of one person to another.* A Level 3 person doesn't view sex *only* as something that makes him "feel good" or as something that makes him "feel desirable." He looks *outside of himself* and considers the needs and the future of the other person.

Furthermore, a Level 3 person recognizes that a sexual relationship must be *exclusive* in order to be healthy. Having more than one sexual partner can cause people to focus more on themselves and their own desires, rather than what is good for the other person. This makes it easy to fall back into Happiness Level 1 or 2. When that happens, trust breaks down. It is very difficult to trust someone when you think that person cares more about himself than about you.

When someone forms a sexual bond with more than one person, it can lead to comparisons, jealousy, heightened self-consciousness, and even aggression and possessiveness. When that happens, a person really cannot have *intimacy* any more. This is one reason why a committed, lifelong marriage is the *only* healthy and truly safe place for sexuality to occur. In an

ATTAIN A HIGHER LEVEL OF HAPPINESS BY DEVELOPING A DEEPER VIEW OF LOVE.

Use the lines on this page to write down examples of married couples who have turned their love into a **generous** union that gives to others beyond the marriage. You can use examples from movies, television, music, people in the news, history, literature, or your life.

exclusive Level 3 relationship (marriage), sexual intimacy becomes part of the gift that two people share with one another.

Some people argue that you can have an exclusive relationship *without* being married. That may be possible, but without a marriage vow, there is no real commitment to be exclusive, and there is no commitment that it will be permanent.

Why is this such a big deal? Because two people who are in a so-called "exclusive" sexual relationship without a lifelong commitment will not be able to give all of themselves to one another. By refusing to commit their *futures* to each other, they are holding back a big part of themselves. When they do this, they lose the foundation for trust that is necessary to be truly intimate.

Although *sexual intimacy* should be shared with only one other person in marriage, this does *not* mean that the couple's love should be selfish. While a married couple's sexual intimacy should be permanently exclusive, their *love* should not be. One characteristic of Love 3 is that it always *moves beyond itself*. By giving themselves to each other as a gift, a married couple forms a *new union*. In the words of Jesus Christ, "The two shall become one" (Mark 10:8). This new union also has to move beyond itself. So in a truly healthy marriage, the "gift of myself to you" becomes a "gift of ourselves to others."

There are many ways that a married couple can do this. For example, they can welcome children into their family, engage in mission work together, and invite friends and neighbors to share in holiday celebrations. The husband might support his wife when she wants to become a nurse in order to save lives. The wife might support her husband when he wants to become a counselor to help struggling families. As you can see from these examples, a couple with a healthy Level 3 love will use their union to do even more good *together* than they could have done *alone*.

On the other hand, it is easy to tell when a married couple has turned their love into a selfish union. They become so completely involved in *their* activities and *their* things that they don't seem to have time or room in their lives for anyone else. When they are with their friends, they give each other little winks and "love signals." They have their own special language and love messages. You almost feel like they have their own secret club, and that you are an outsider. Instead of feeling welcome in their presence, you feel like you are intruding. After only five or ten minutes you're looking for an excuse to leave. As a teenager, you may have experienced this same thing with certain friends who are attracted to each other, and when you are around them, they make you feel like you don't even exist.

AGAPE IN LOVE 3

If you think that Love 3 sounds a lot like *agape*, you would be correct. To a person in Level 3, *agape* is the meaning of life, so it is much more attractive to Level 3 people than it is to Level 1 and 2 people. In fact, the goal of a Level 3 person is to make *agape* the most important kind of love, and to let the other three kinds of love be guided by *agape*.

© 101PHOTO/ iStockphoto

Write a short scenario in which a couple turns their love into a **selfish** union that excludes others and focuses only on their own desires, fulfillment, and gratification. Your story can be fictional or historical. Explain why the union is selfish.

LOVE 4

Happiness Level 4 is the fulfillment that comes from surrendering one's heart and life to God. For some, the idea of surrendering one's heart and life to anybody is very unattractive. One may ask, "Why would I want to worship a God who requires me to surrender to Him? Isn't that oppressive and controlling?"

From a Level 4 perspective, if God is Love, then surrendering to God is not like surrendering to an enemy during a war. Surrendering to God would include letting go of selfish desires, asking God to help us accept His unconditional Love, and following Him by imitating that kind of love. In Level 4, a person surrenders his heart and life to God *because* he believes that God is absolute Truth, unconditional Love, perfect Justice, perfect Beauty, and perfect Unity. He believes that God wants to share this goodness, and that He can and will fulfill our deepest desires for all of eternity.

If this is who God is, then God's purpose cannot be to control and manipulate human beings. For what good would it do for Him to manipulate people? How would it accomplish His objectives? Manipulation and control lead to resentment and rebellion, not to love. God's purpose is to show us how to gain control over our lives so that we are no longer dominated by greed, selfishness, anger, pride, fear, jealousy, and hatred. He wants to make us free to love, but He cannot do that unless we first let Him into our lives. God patiently waits for us to *invite* Him in—all the while loving us and pulling at our hearts with His gentle voice. He will do whatever it takes to show us that He loves us, that His purpose is for *our* greatest good, and that we can trust Him. But He won't take away our freedom by forcing Himself on us, for that would be contrary to love.

When we invite God in and surrender to the love that makes us free, the Holy Spirit begins the process of awakening and inspiring us. We may begin to notice that we take more of an interest in what is happening at church. We might find ourselves more interested in religious questions, and may want to be more active in church life. We may become more attracted to friends who have faith and who

If you are interested in deepening Love 4 in your life, what steps can you take that will help invite God in? What specifically would you like to do differently?

want to deepen their own love and commitment in the same way.

We might think that these new interests are completely of our own making, but many people find that in looking back, they were being led, inspired, and enchanted by the Holy Spirit. This began a journey that led them to deeper prayer, reflection, church commitment, and selection of friends, and this brought them to a kind of transformation that they did not anticipate or even know existed. They were being deepened in love—specifically *agape*.

When we love others in Level 4, we recognize that God desires every human being to the same degree, and that His purpose is for *everyone* to surrender their hearts and lives to Him. His objective is to share perfect Truth, Love, Justice, Beauty, and Unity with *all* human beings, and He is capable of fulfilling all human desires for eternity, so long as we invite Him in. God creates everyone with the *freedom* to invite Him in or to reject Him, and He will not go where He is not invited. The knowledge of this freedom, purpose, and destiny in others causes a Level 4 person to want to love every human being as a precious and irreplaceable treasure.

Notice that Love 4 is not a vague "love of humanity." For example, it would not be Love 4 to think: "I love humanity—but I find that *people* irritate me. So I'll do something good for humanity, such as preserve natural resources for future generations, as long as I don't have to deal with actual human beings." In Love 4, there isn't merely a sentimental love of "humanity in general." Love 4 includes the deepest possible love for *each and every unique and individual real human being*, because one sees the great potential for good that every person has.

At times, it can be difficult to love individual human beings, especially when they are using *their* freedom to do things that are destructive, harmful, or evil. But Scripture says, "love your enemies, do good to those who hate you" (Luke 6:27). This is easier to do when we recall that every human being is created with the freedom to choose good. When we love an individual who is doing evil, it isn't the *evil* we are loving—it is the *person* underneath the evil, who has the ability to turn around, reject evil, and do good. We *know* that ability is still there and that the true purpose of that person's life is to choose goodness. That is what we love.

In short, Love 4 is recognizing the unconditional love that God has for us and for every other human being, and responding to that love. When a Level 4 person sees how much God loves her, it moves her to love Him. And when she sees how much He loves each and every human being, it moves her to love them as well.

LOVE YOUR ENEMIES, DO GOOD TO THOSE WHO HATE YOU. (LUKE 6:27)

Moving to Level 4 after a lifetime of focusing on Levels 1 through 3 can be excruciatingly difficult. The journey can be made more accessible by breaking it into five steps:

1] **I recognize that my life has dignity** because I am called to perfect love with God.

2] I become aware that I am not the only one who has this dignity. **Every other human being is infinitely precious and lovable to God**. These other persons need and desire perfect Truth, Love, Justice, Beauty, and Unity just as I do. This allows me to have even deeper empathy, understanding, and respect for other individual human beings.

3] I realize that since I am not perfect, **I cannot *perfectly* fulfill all the desires of any human being** (including myself).

4] **The only person who can *perfectly* fulfill any human is God**. No human being can ever be satisfied with anything short of the presence of God.

5] We are all linked to each other, and to God. In a very real sense, we are all family members. We are responsible for each other. **Since I want everyone to be perfectly fulfilled, I try to help others find God, and then I move aside and allow God to become the center of their lives.**

This five-step process can help lead us directly into Love 4. If you would like to move more deeply into Love 4, think about each separate step, and write down your own thoughts about moving through them. What can you do to work toward each step?

The next section will make clear how the four *kinds* of love (*storge*, *philia*, *eros*, and *agape*) can each be experienced in the fourth level of love.

STORGE IN LOVE 4

Storge is a spontaneous feeling of affection and delight. People who choose Level 4 as their dominant desire can certainly experience this, and perhaps in a more satisfying way than people in the other three levels. Since Level 4 makes us aware that God wants what is best for us (and other people), each experience of *storge* can be seen as a gift from God, and can lead to gratitude.

What would *storge* look like in Level 4? Imagine that your friend Jack invites you over to his house for a party with a small group of friends. You're excited because you need a break after a long week of exams, and Jack happens to be one of the funniest people you've ever met. He always has an inexhaustible supply of jokes, and his facial expressions and body language are hysterical. You go to the party, and just as you expected, Jack has everyone laughing until their stomachs hurt. Afterwards, you're walking home and you realize how good you feel because you spent all afternoon laughing. All the stress of exams seems to just melt away. Suddenly you become aware of a deep feeling of *gratitude* for what you just experienced. You whisper a quick prayer: "Lord, thank you for giving my buddy Jack the ability to make everyone forget about their worries and just feel better." That's *storge* in Level 4.

PHILIA IN LOVE 4

Philia refers to a friendship in which you have a common interest with the other person, and you expect things from one another in this relationship. If you are focused on Level 4, your ability to have healthy *philia* relationships will be stronger. Even though you have expectations of each other, you don't expect one another to be God, so there is room for understanding and forgiveness. You also see the friendship as an opportunity to help each other grow closer to God. These types of friendships tend to be the strongest because both people in the friendship believe that the other has their very best interests at heart.

For example, imagine you are thinking to yourself: "I'm lonely, and I'd really like to invite my friend Sue over to watch a movie at my house. But I've had her over twice in the last two weeks, and she has never invited me. Forget it. I am not going to invite her over." This attitude assumes the worst in Sue, and does not show any concern about her as a person. Sue will eventually figure out that the friendship is shallow, and will feel downhearted about it. Meanwhile, you are feeling downhearted because you are keeping a scorecard about who gets invited more often, and you are losing.

In a Level 4 mindset, the thought process would be elevated: "It's strange that Sue never invites me to her house to hang out. But I know

she cares about me, so there's got to be a reason. I've heard her say that her parents argue a lot. Maybe she doesn't want me over at her house because she's afraid I'll hear them arguing." You might decide to say a quick prayer, "*God, I'll invite Sue over, and if talking about it will be good for her, then please show me an opportunity to bring it up.*" Notice that this attitude is all about Sue, and has her best interests at heart. If Sue is also a Level 3 or 4 person, the friendship is certain to grow.

EROS IN LOVE 4

A Level 4 attitude about love takes sexuality to its highest and most fulfilling level.

If a person's vocation is to be married and he is operating out of Love 4, he would not pursue an *eros* relationship simply to satisfy a sexual desire or to "own" his beloved. Rather, he would see his beloved through the "eyes of Love 4," and would recognize that God loves her *even more than he does*. He will see that God has a plan for his beloved and for her future. This knowledge will give him a strong sense of *humility*, because he will want the relationship to be part of fulfilling God's plan for his beloved, rather than pulling her off course. There is freedom in loving and being loved in this way.

As people begin looking for a spouse, it is natural to develop a powerful desire for a sexual relationship with those to whom we are attracted. Sexual desire is good. However, in Love 4, the desire is controlled by a deeper desire to live according to God's plan: "Lord, you are wiser than

© alexxx1981 / iStockphoto

I am. I trust your judgment more than my own. *I want your judgment to control this attraction.*"

This prayer or reflection requires humility. It can produce powerful results, because it allows you to see beyond your own immediate wants, and consider the situation through the eyes of God. In the case of sexual attraction, you can step outside of yourself and ask: "Would God really want us to have a sexual relationship when we haven't made a commitment to love and care for each other in a lifelong, permanent, exclusive relationship (marriage)? Would God really treat something as important as sex that casually?"

Then, turning to your own situation, you might ask: "If I don't feel ready to make a permanent, public commitment to love and cherish this person exclusively for the rest of my life, is it fair for me to ask this person to give me the immensely powerful gift of sexual intimacy? Is that what God would want for *me*? Or does He have something better in mind—something *enduring*, something *deeper*, something that looks more like *His* design for love?"

This kind of questioning can lead to *better knowledge* of yourself, *better vision* of the person you love, and *better wisdom* about your relationship and how it fits into God's plan for both of your lives.

AGAPE IN LOVE 4

Agape is selfless love. People who choose Level 4 as dominant believe that *agape* is the meaning of life. But more than this, they believe that *perfect Agape* exists—and that perfect *Agape* is God. God is **perfect** patience, kindness, forgiveness, empathy, self-sacrifice, care, concern, compassion, gentleness, and humility. He is perfect Love, and He calls us to accept His perfect Love and to imitate it.

To be sure, *agape* requires a great deal of work and sacrifice. To a person in Level 4, it is worth the effort, but it can still be difficult to achieve. Scripture offers hundreds of examples of *agape* that help us to trust that God is love, and to learn how to imitate Him. For example, read the passage on love in 1 Corinthians 13:4-8. This passage is sometimes called the *Hymn to Love* and is printed in full on the next page.

Hymn to Love

Think about it: What would your life be like if you put your name in place of "love" in the *Hymn to Love* on this page? How would your actions and attitudes be different than they are now?

Hymn to Love 1 Corinthians 13:4-8	If it is true that God is unconditional Love, we can translate the verse like this:
Love is patient	God is *infinitely* patient
Love is kind	God is *perfectly* kind
It does not envy	God *never* envies
It does not boast	He *never* boasts
It is not proud	He is *never* proud
It is not rude	God is *never* rude
It is not self-seeking	He is *never* self-seeking
It is not easily angered	He is *absolutely not* an "angry God"
It keeps no record of wrongs	He does not keep an *eternal* record of wrongs
Love does not delight in evil	God *never* delights in evil
Love rejoices in the truth	He *eternally* rejoices with the truth
It always protects	God *always and completely* protects
Always trusts	He *always and totally* entrusts us with what is good
Always hopes	He *always and absolutely* wants what is best for us
Always perseveres	He *always* seeks us
Love never fails	God *never, ever* fails us

I am patient... I am kind...

CONCLUSION

Moving our hearts into Love 3 and 4 is not easy, and doesn't happen overnight. It takes time and work. It can sometimes be frustrating, challenging, and difficult. But if we persevere in trying to love ourselves and others through *agape*, we will learn to love in a far more mature and fulfilling way than we did as children. The love of little children is beautiful because it is innocent and trusting. But it is also selfish. Just ask anyone who has a very young brother or sister. The focus of little children is nearly always on what they get out of the relationship. If we continue loving in this way as adults, we will miss out on the deepest and most beautiful part of relationships with other people and with God.

If you are uncertain about this, you might try *agape* for a period of time – perhaps six or eight weeks. If the exercise becomes difficult, stay with it. It generally takes about six weeks for a new habit to form, and for people to begin to see real changes in the way they are acting and how they feel and think about themselves and others.

Then, think about how you can make an *"agape* difference" in the culture. Our culture cannot be changed unless many of us—including you—are willing to become a tool to help bring about that change.

HOW CAN YOU HELP MOVE THE CULTURE INTO HIGHER VIEWS OF LOVE?

Many young people, and even older people, are deceived by Level 1 and 2 definitions of love. We are surrounded by messages that tell us: "Love is a chemical," "Love is a feeling," "Love is a physical attraction," and "Love is all about you."

As you become an adult, think about ways that you can help move the culture into Level 3 and 4 views of love. Your contribution is extremely important. Perhaps you will become a musician or an artist who creates works that inspire others to be humble, gentle, kind, forgiving, or compassionate. Perhaps you will be an author and write about real or fictional heroes who offered little or great acts of Love 3 or Love 4. Perhaps you will become a mother or a father, and set good examples for virtue, generosity, and self-sacrifice. Perhaps you will become a teacher, a religious, or a public figure, who can have an impact on a great number of people.

Whatever you choose to do with your future, consider the benefits of placing *agape* at the center of your life. The legacy you leave in the world will be greater than anything else you could have otherwise accomplished.

Log onto the website: Principlesandchoices.com for two inspirational examples of *agape* in Love 4. Use code **PCS133** to read how the different names God uses for Himself reveals His unconditional Love. Use code **PCS134** to see God's amazing love through a powerful retelling of the Prodigal Son story.

Use **PCS135** to access vocabulary and other study tools for this chapter

Use the lined space to make a list of social issues you care about, and compare your list with those from other students.

CRIME, RACISM, MARRIAGE, GUN RIGHTS, CLONING, DRUG LAWS, IMMIGRATION, WAR, TERRORISM, ABORTION, POVERTY, CAPITAL PUNISHMENT, RELIGIOUS FREEDOM, ASSISTED SUICIDE, EUTHANASIA...

WHAT'S RIGHT? WHAT'S WRONG?

© Beboy / Fotolia

CHAPTER 4: APPLICATION TO SOCIAL ISSUES

Social issues are concerns that affect many members of society. They are usually controversial, and deal with questions of right and wrong (moral or ethical issues). They can include diverse topics such as crime, racism, the definition of marriage, gun rights, discrimination, drug laws, immigration, and capital punishment. All of these topics are important, and the list can include many other issues as well.

At the end of this chapter, you can apply the principles learned in this book to any social issue. Here we will examine **abortion** and **assisted suicide**, which deal with the very beginning and the very end of life. These two issues provide an opportunity to see all of the principles in action.

In the public debate on abortion and assisted suicide, those who are against these acts are generally referred to as "pro-life." **Pro-life** is the position that all human beings, including the unborn, the elderly, the terminally ill, and the disabled, have intrinsic dignity and worth, and should be protected by law. To be pro-life means to believe that abortion, euthanasia, and assisted suicide should be against the law because these acts are unjust, unethical, and contrary to Level 3 and Level 4 principles.

Those who hold that the practices of abortion, euthanasia, and assisted suicide should be legal are generally referred to as "**pro-choice**." This position holds that not all human beings are full human persons, that not all human beings are worthy of protection under the law, and/or that killing an innocent human person can sometimes be justified and should be legal.

This chapter will take a Level 3 and Level 4 perspective, and will argue that those higher viewpoints require a pro-life response to abortion. Most people understand **what** pro-life people think about abortion and assisted suicide; but many are not familiar with **why**. As was mentioned at the beginning of this book, this course will give the reader an opportunity to fully examine the reasons. The student is encouraged to seek wisdom on these issues by asking questions, testing answers, challenging assertions, and posing counter-arguments.

Some questions that may be raised in your mind or in class can be answered only by using principles that will be discussed in the two later volumes of this book series. For example, on the issue of abortion you may ask: "What if the mother's life is in danger?" or "Is the embryo a human person or an undifferentiated blob of cells?" These questions, and many others, will be addressed in the later books. At this point, we will assume that the fetus *is* a person, and that the mother's life is *not* in imminent danger. These assumptions will allow us to focus on the principles we have discussed thus far. Those principles will create a foundation upon which we can build other principles that will answer the questions above.

KEY TERMS

autonomy

euthanasia

induced abortion

Level 3 and 4 Principles

miscarriage

physician-assisted suicide

principle

pro-life

sacrifice

social issues

spontaneous abortion

You can get help applying these principles to other social justice issues by referring to a document published by the Pontifical Council on Justice and Peace entitled: *Compendium of the Social Doctrine of the Church*. Use code **PCS141**.

Post your comments and ask questions on our Facebook page. Check out the latest videos on the YouTube channel. Get more information and answers on the website. Find all the URLs at the front and back of this textbook on the "Check It Out" pages.

LEVEL 3 AND 4 PRINCIPLES

There are six basic principles that can be deduced from the first three chapters of this book. We refer to them as **Level 3 and 4 principles** because they derive from Level 3 and 4 definitions about happiness, meaning, and purpose in life. Individuals who prioritize Levels 3 and 4 will find these principles to be essential.

An individual's decision to accept or reject the following principles will have a profound impact on whether that person's life will be focused on others or focused only on the self, and will affect whether that person works to build community and foster peace and justice, or contributes to the deterioration of those goods.

PRINCIPLE #1:

Happiness 3 (contributing to the good of others) and 4 (surrender to the God of love) are the highest goods a human can attain, because these objectives allow us to achieve our fullest potential. They lead to greater personal happiness than Levels 1 and 2 (physical pleasure and ego-gratification).

PRINCIPLE #2:

Levels 1 and 2 are not intrinsically evil and should be pursued in their proper proportion. However, if we subordinate Level 3 and 4 goals to Level 1 and 2 desires, we risk our own happiness by falling short of our full potential. It is good to avoid the temptation to misuse Levels 1 and 2 by practicing **virtues** like prudence, justice, temperance, and courage.

PRINCIPLE #3:

Success is not defined by the material things we own, nor by how intelligent, talented, beautiful, or physically fit we are. It is defined by the degree to which we are unattached to those things and striving to make a difference to other people or build the kingdom of God.

PRINCIPLE #4:

The highest **quality of life** is experienced in the love of others (human and divine). It is not measured by the degree to which we experience material wealth or ego-gratification.

PRINCIPLE #5:

Love looks for what is ultimately good for the other person and for the kingdom of God, over and above our own Level 1, 2, and 3 desires. This attitude directs and complements how we love ourselves. ("Love your neighbor as yourself." —Mark 12:31)

PRINCIPLE #6:

All of the principles above can be summarized in the principle that Jesus taught in Matthew 7:12 and Luke 6:31, known as the **Golden Rule**: "Do unto others as you would have them do unto you." (By this, Jesus means, "Do good to others.")

We can now apply these six principles to the issues of abortion and euthanasia, and explore their implications.

ABORTION

A general definition of abortion is "an intentional act which ends a pregnancy by directly or indirectly causing the death of an embryo or fetus." This is also called an **induced abortion**. The word "induced" means that someone intentionally caused the abortion to happen.

A **spontaneous abortion** occurs when an embryo or fetus dies not by an intentional act, but as the unintended natural result of a problem in the pregnancy, or because something traumatic took place such as a fall or a car accident. When the baby dies, the mother's body will usually trigger contractions, expelling the baby. Occasionally, the baby does not come out, and medical professionals must help remove the deceased child in order to prevent harm to the mother. Medical professionals often call this procedure an "abortion," but it is a different kind of abortion. The pro-life position does not oppose this medical procedure because it does not cause the death of the baby—the child has already died.

Spontaneous abortions are also called "miscarriages." Miscarriages are unintended events. Their occurrence is not a controversial social issue, so they will not be addressed here. This section will focus only on induced abortions. In the next section, we will use the logic, principles, and insight from the previous three chapters to answer some of the most common arguments in favor of legal abortion, and to make the case against abortion.

Actual 20-week old unborn child

© Life Issues Institute

"Abortion is necessary for women to find happiness and fulfillment."

One common argument in favor of abortion is the assumption that abortion is necessary for women to advance their careers, fulfill educational goals, or pursue other dreams. The claim is that without abortion, women cannot find happiness.

However, polls by Gallup consistently find that a majority of Americans (both men *and* women) hold that abortion is "morally wrong," and 64% of women believe that abortion should be illegal in all or most circumstances. It is reasonable to assume that these millions of women (and millions of men) do not wish to deny women happiness or interfere with their dreams. **Obviously, when**

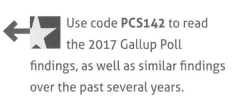

Use code **PCS142** to read the 2017 Gallup Poll findings, as well as similar findings over the past several years.

the claim is made that "abortion is necessary for women to find happiness," the definition of "happiness" matters a great deal.

Imagine an advocacy organization that believes **racial discrimination** should be legal because it is necessary in order for the dominant race in their community to pursue happiness and fulfill their dreams. The organization argues, "If our constituency is not preferred over people of other colors, they may not be able to get into the colleges they want, or get the career advancements they need. They may make less money and suffer economically. People who are opposed to racial discrimination want to deny our constituents happiness and destroy their dreams."

We would immediately recognize the shallowness and illegitimacy of the argument, and would challenge the way this organization is defining happiness. To racially discriminate against one group of people in order to advance another person's college education or career is to be rooted in a Level 1 and Level 2 view of happiness that embodies selfishness, superiority, contempt for others, and profound injustice.

Principle #1 holds that Levels 3 and 4 lead to greater happiness than Levels 1 and 2. If we see merit in this principle, then people will *never* find true happiness when they harm others in order to pursue their own Level 1 and Level 2 goals. It may be true that racial discrimination could help some people achieve Level 1

ARE YOU WILLING TO TREAT OTHERS UNJUSTLY IN ORDER TO GET AHEAD IN LIFE?

or Level 2 happiness, such as more money, power, advancement, etc. But discrimination could never help someone achieve Level 3 or 4 happiness, because Levels 3 and 4 advocate for treating all human beings equally and fairly, out of love and respect. Racial discrimination is unjust and detracts from this goal.

It is not wrong to want a good education, a good job, and a good income. There is nothing wrong with the Level 1 and Level 2 happiness that comes from enjoying these things. However, **Principle #2** is critical for maintaining balance. Whenever Level 1 and 2 goals hijack Level 3 and 4 goals, we risk our own happiness by falling short of our full potential. It is best to avoid this temptation by practicing virtue. Discriminating against one group of people in order to fulfill one's dreams defeats the whole meaning and purpose of human life.

Furthermore, laws are made to protect those who are weak, and to help people reach their highest potential. Since racial discrimination causes people to pursue what is unworthy of us by harming other people in order to fulfill lower levels of happiness, it should be against the law.

It would seem that if Level 3 and Level 4 people are going to be consistent, they must reject the argument that abortion is justified because it assists women in finding happiness and fulfillment.

Setting goals for the future, such as a college education, is

THE WORDS WE USE

In this chapter, we use the terms "killing children," "killing unborn babies," and "killing people" in reference to abortion. Some abortion activists have tried to censor the use of these words, claiming that such terms are inflammatory. However, to ban the use of accurate words because some people feel uncomfortable with them is unfair and counterproductive. People who support abortion should use the words that are necessary to explain why they think that way. They should extend the same courtesy to people who are opposed to abortion, without trying to censor the very words that are necessary for an honest dialogue on the subject. Since there is no disagreement on either side that abortion terminates the life of a developing being with a full human genome, and since "killing" is an accurate and more common way of saying the same thing, we use this term. We do not use the word "terminate" because it lacks sufficient meaning. You will notice, however, that we also do not use the word "murder." This is because "murder" is a legal term that labels killing which is forbidden by law. Since abortion is legal, the term would not be technically accurate.

good—especially if the motivation is to help other people and to make our lives more meaningful. But to kill another human being now (in an abortion) in order to stay in school so that we can help other people in the future is a contradiction. It defeats the whole purpose of wanting to make a positive difference with our lives.

Killing people in order to follow our dreams will never lead to Happiness Levels 3 and 4. At most, it might lead to an increase in Level 1 and 2 happiness. But if human beings are made for love, then sacrificing Levels 3 and 4 in favor of Levels 1 and 2 will inevitably lead to unhappiness. And it becomes clear that legally allowing one group of people to kill another group of people for Level 1 and Level 2 motivations is unjust.

At this point, there is often introduced the mistaken argument that most abortions occur because the pregnant mother is ill, or her unborn child is ill; or because she has been the victim of rape or incest. According to the Guttmacher Institute, a research organization that supports legal abortion, only 4% of women who have abortions choose it because of concerns about their health, 3% because of concerns that the baby might have a health problem, and less than one half of one percent (0.5%) because they were raped.

The Guttmacher study found that more than 90% of abortions are chosen for reasons such as not wanting a child (or another child), concerns about the financial costs, believing the child would interfere with their education, career, or a relationship, or feeling that the timing is wrong.**D**

If you are a Level 3 or Level 4 person, these statistics should concern you. The vast majority of abortions are chosen for Level 1 and Level 2 reasons—reasons that are about money, career, education, or other concerns that put the *self* above the *life of another human being.*

Adding to this problem, most women in the studies reported that they were pressured into these selfish concerns by someone else, such as a boyfriend, spouse, parent, teacher, coach, boss, or abortion provider. In

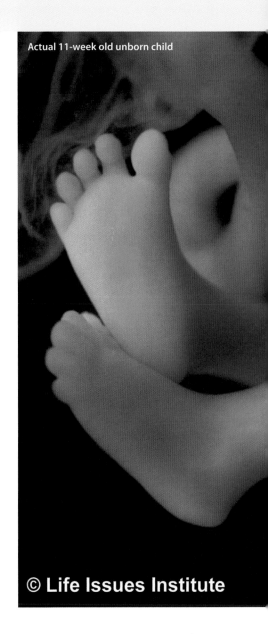

Actual 11-week old unborn child

© Life Issues Institute

other words, women are being pressured into choosing abortion for Level 1 or 2 reasons, above their own Level 3 and Level 4 maternal instincts to protect and nurture their child.

According to recent studies:[E]

> 64% of women having abortions said they felt pressured or coerced to abort,

> 84% said they were not fully informed,

> 52% felt rushed before the abortion, and

> 54% felt uncertain beforehand.

When women choose abortion against their Level 3 and Level 4 maternal instincts, it usually leads to severe **un**happiness. Several scientific studies have shown that among women who have had an abortion:

> suicide rates are six times higher compared to women who give birth,[F]

> 65% suffer symptoms of Post-Traumatic Stress Disorder[G] (which can include depression, nightmares, anxiety, guilt,

suicidal thoughts, re-living the abortion, eating disorders, and drug or alcohol abuse),

> the risk of clinical depression is 65% higher,[H]

> 60% said "part of me died" after the abortion,[I]

> drug and alcohol abuse significantly increase,[J]

> there are significantly higher rates of psychiatric treatment,[K]

> the risk of domestic violence and relationship problems increases,[L]

> there is a 60% increased risk of later miscarriage,[M]

> 31% suffer health complications after abortion,[N]

> and there is a 62% higher risk of death (from any cause, such as accident, homicide, or suicide) after abortion.[O]

These scientific studies show that the claim that "abortion is necessary for women to find happiness and fulfillment" is very deceptive. It assumes that happiness is only about getting a job, making money, and following our

© AndyL / iStockphoto

most intense momentary desires. But when women get abortions and go on to pursue their dreams, the statistics show that they are overwhelmingly NOT happy. This is because the deceptive claim completely ignores that all human beings were created for a deeper happiness that comes from sacrificing our needs and wants for the needs of others—such as an unborn child who is very weak, vulnerable, voiceless, and dependent on us for survival.

Giving up personal goals in order to take care of someone else who is weak and vulnerable makes most people feel noble and honorable. But the statistics reveal that rejecting, neglecting, or abandoning someone who is weak and vulnerable in order to pursue personal goals makes most people feel guilty and ashamed. This is because human beings are made for love. Our hearts know when we have betrayed our deepest meaning and purpose in life.

When men and women choose to sacrifice education, employment opportunities, or material goods in order to attend to the needs of a child (born or unborn), this heroic and selfless attitude deserves our support.

Some people feel that they cannot afford to put off college or work to tend to a pregnancy or a child. The good news is that we live in a time and a culture in which men and women do not have to choose between saving the life of their baby and saving their education or careers. There are a multitude of organizations and programs that can help individuals to graduate and earn livable wages without having to kill their own children. A society that offers abortion as the only way to achieve these goals is not only cruel and unjust, it is also unrealistic and narrow-minded.

"Abortion increases opportunities for success."

This argument suggests that abortion will lead to greater success by making it easier for pregnant women to finish school, advance their careers, and earn a comfortable salary. The weakness of this argument can be seen in the discussion above about happiness. Once again, it depends on

Listen to the stories of real women who became unexpectedly pregnant under difficult circumstances, and sought abortions. Find out how their lives were transformed and their dreams fulfilled when they chose to set aside their personal concerns and choose life for their children. Use codes **PCS144** and **PCS145**.

what you mean by "success." People who are willing to sacrifice their own dreams for the sake of another human being often feel *more* successful than when they were pursuing their own educational or career goals, or spending money on things they wanted.

Recall that Principle #3 holds that true "success" is about making a difference to other people (Level 3) and allowing God's unconditional Love into your life (Level 4). If you agree with that, then success cannot be defined by how many things you own, or by how smart, talented, beautiful, or able-bodied you are.

Abortion advocates frequently claim that if abortion becomes illegal, women will lose opportunities for success. Principle #3 shows how misleading this argument is. It completely belittles the contributions made by parents who believe their greatest accomplishment was giving life to their children and raising them with love. It also ignores the fact that there are many ways to pursue your dreams without having to kill your own children.

Sometimes when people use the success argument to support abortion, they aren't referring to the success of the mother or the father. They're referring to the *baby's* chances of success in life. Some people believe that abortion should be legal if, during the pregnancy, the unborn baby is diagnosed with a **disability, a serious illness, or a defect**. They claim these children can never be successful. The first major problem with this attitude is that these diagnoses are frequently wrong—which means that abortion

would kill a perfectly healthy baby.

Secondly, and more importantly, it is a myth that people cannot be successful just because they are disabled. We wouldn't say that to an *adult* person with a disability, so why is it acceptable to say it about someone who is *unborn* with a disability? The fact that he is small and dependent is all the more reason why we should be protecting him from people who would have him killed.

Just because people cannot do things in the same way you can does not mean they cannot have a successful life. The composer Ludwig van Beethoven was deaf; the famous physicist Stephen Hawking is quadriplegic; Franklin Delano Roosevelt (the 32nd President of the United States of America) had polio and was confined to a wheelchair his entire life; the Hollywood actor Tom Cruise is severely dyslexic. These people have accomplished amazing things with their lives, despite their disabilities.

In extreme cases, there are some people born with disabilities that are so severe that they actually cannot do many physical or mental activities like walking, talking, and responding to others. However, recall that Principle #3 holds that true success does not come from our physical or mental abilities. It comes from making a positive difference to other people, and surrendering to God's Love. The more we make a positive difference to others and the more we surrender to God, the more free we are to find true success.

SUCCESS CAN NOT BE GAINED BY HARMING OTHERS.

Claudia's Story

I was 41 years old when I became pregnant with my first child. When my husband and I went to the doctor for our first visit, we were stunned by the nervous reactions of the medical staff. Over and over again, we were told that the risk of having a disabled child increases with the age of the mother. We were offered many tests to try to detect whether our baby had any disabilities. When one test revealed that we had a very high chance of giving birth to a child with Down Syndrome, we were offered "genetic counseling" to discuss our "options."

It was as if everyone assumed that my husband and I couldn't possibly love a "less than biologically perfect" child. We were appalled. So when I finally said, "Well, what if we love this baby regardless of whether or not she is genetically normal?" the technician said, "Oh, well then you don't need the genetic counseling." In other words, the counseling was just about getting rid of our baby.

What kind of people have we become that we would pressure parents to find out if there's a chance that their child is "imperfect" so that they can hurry up and have her killed before it's too late? Whatever happened to unconditional love?

Several months later we gave birth to a healthy baby girl with no Down Syndrome. Good thing her parents loved her no matter what.

Where is the evidence that persons with severe physical or mental disabilities cannot make a positive difference to other people? Where is the evidence that they cannot surrender everything to God? In fact, many disabled people find that it is easier to focus on what is really important in life—such as family, friends, love, generosity, patience, and putting their faith in God—*because* of their disability.

What about the argument that some disabled people are very unhappy with their lives and wish they had never been born? No doubt there are some disabled people who feel that way. But there are also many able-bodied people who are very unhappy with their lives, and who wish they had never been born. There is no way to predict in the womb who is going to end up feeling successful in life, and who is going to end up feeling like a failure. So why is it acceptable to make judgments against disabled people when they are unborn, to assume that they would not want to live, and to kill them? How do we know what they would want? It is virtually unheard of that people with Down Syndrome and similar developmental disabilities kill themselves or even express the desire to kill themselves.

Is it not the worst kind of discrimination and arrogance to assume that someone else would not want to live? Doesn't this attitude toward disabled persons actually reveal our own Level 1 and Level 2 attitudes about life? Many people with disabilities think that the *judgmental and negative attitudes* that others have toward persons with disabilities reveals a far more profound disability than anything they suffer from.

Search online for true stories of disabled people who have made remarkable Level 1, 2, 3, and 4 achievements despite their disabilities. Use code **PCS147** to watch a news report about Diane Rose, a woman from Waco, Texas, who sews extraordinary quilts — despite the fact that she is totally blind! Use code **PCS148** to see the inspirational video about a man born without arms or legs.

Mother Teresa (now known as Saint Teresa of Calcutta) was a Catholic nun who lived in Calcutta, India, and took care of tens of thousands of the poorest and sickest people on earth for over 45 years. But she once said that America is the poorest country in the world because we do not know how to love. She said, "It is a great poverty to decide that a child must die so that you may live as you wish." What did she mean by this?

Use code **PCS1492** to read an excerpt from a speech given by Mother Teresa. **Then write down your own thoughts about quality of life in the space provided here.**

"Abortion is necessary if the baby would not have a good quality of life, or if the family would have a lower quality of life because of his birth."

When people make this argument, we would do well to ask the question, "What do you mean by 'quality of life?'" Usually, they are referring to the condition of being disabled or poor. But having a disability doesn't mean someone is going to have a low quality of life, and neither does being poor—unless one is defining quality of life only by Levels 1 and 2.

If we believe that quality of life is experienced only through physical health and material wealth, then the less of these things we have, the more likely we are to think we have a low quality of life. But if we believe that a greater quality of life can be achieved by giving and receiving faith, hope, and love, and all of the virtues that go along with them, then health and wealth will have little to do with whether or not we think we have a high quality of life.

This doesn't mean that we shouldn't tend to Level 1 and 2 needs. Poverty, illness, and disabilities can be serious burdens for the people who suffer them, and everyone has a responsibility to help ease their burdens. But killing unborn people because they might be born poor, ill, disabled, or with a physical defect makes no more sense than executing teenagers or adults who have the same conditions because we judge them to have a "low quality of life."

There are several other important points to be made here: (1) One person should never presume to judge the worthiness of another person's quality of life. (2) Being born poor does not necessarily mean that a person is forever condemned to poverty. (3) Being born disabled does not mean a person cannot participate in any of the activities that add quality to life. (4) Consider which of the following is truly compassionate—helping people reach a better quality of life, or killing people who are vulnerable because we judge their lives to be without value?

Another side of the "quality of life" argument is the claim that abortion is justifiable for babies who are diagnosed with terminal illnesses. After all, they are going to die anyway, so what kind of quality of life can they possibly have?

"What may look like compassion to some people looks more like contempt to many of us with disabilities who have too often heard that someone else thinks we would be better off dead."

— *Diane Coleman, president of the disability rights group Not Dead Yet*

In answer to this: (1) It is very difficult for doctors to predict precisely when someone is going to die, and they are frequently wrong. Patients often outlive their doctors' expectations – sometimes by many years.

(2) It is a great injustice to condemn someone to death because "they are going to die anyway." *You* are going to die someday, too. That would *not* be a good excuse for someone to kill you now.

© anouchka / iStockphoto

Go online and search for articles and true stories of people whom doctors said were going to die, but then they didn't, or they lived much longer than anyone thought. You can include stories of unborn children. Use code **PCS1494** to send the links to us and to read real stories that others have submitted. Share what you find on our Facebook page.

"It is not our disability that is the problem, but rather it is the way our disabilities are viewed by others."

— Drexel Deal, chair of the Disabled Persons' Organization

For more quotations like this, use code **PCS1491.**

(3) Recall Mary at the foot of the cross. She knew her son was going to die, but she did not beg the Roman soldiers to "put him out of his misery." She stayed with Jesus and suffered with him, recognizing that his life had a purpose, even to the very end.

(4) Just because someone may soon die does not mean that person cannot experience a high quality of life. Quality of life is not determined by how long we live; it is determined by our experience of love. If every person is loved and wanted by God, then wouldn't every unborn child in some way be able to experience quality of life Level 4—even those who are diagnosed with terminal illnesses and may not live very long? If we worked as hard to love and want every unborn child as some people

work to keep abortion legal, perhaps we could help those children experience true quality of life.

(5) Sometimes the "quality of life" argument is used to justify abortion to protect the quality of life of the other family members—for example, if the family will not be able to financially support another child, or if the mother will suffer health problems because of the pregnancy. But when is it justifiable to kill innocent people in order to improve the living conditions of others?

We would not encourage a poor mother with eight children to kill the oldest three who eat the most. Encouraging her to kill the youngest and most vulnerable child, the one in her womb, is equally irrational.

People suffer from poverty for a variety of reasons. Sometimes they lack the education or the opportunity to succeed. Sometimes they live in an economically depressed area and cannot find adequate jobs. Sometimes they make poor decisions—such as dropping out of school or using drugs — which limit their opportunities later. In some instances, they are oppressed by negligent, greedy, or power-hungry employers or governments. And in other circumstances,

★ Despite what was said on this page about starvation being rare in the United States, it is true that in many developing countries some people are so poor that they do face the possibility of starvation. The commonly accepted "solution" from wealthy nations has been to bring abortion to these poorer countries, and encourage women to abort their children. Can you think of solutions that do *not* involve abortion or other harmful methods?

their nations are torn by war and conflict. Often, those around them who are better off do not provide the assistance and care that they could and should.

Regardless of the reasons for poverty, it is unjust to blame unborn children for the problems that adults create. Furthermore, abortion does not solve any of these problems. Abortion has been legal in most places in the world for over 30 years, yet there is no evidence that it has reduced poverty.

From a quality of life perspective, it is important to consider what we mean by "poverty." It is unheard of that anyone in the Western world starves to death because of having "too many children." It is doubtful that this has ever happened in the United States in contemporary times. Having children can certainly make things economically difficult. If a family has several children, they will usually make many material sacrifices that other families do not have to make. But "poverty" in the United States generally does not mean that anyone will have to starve to death. Our nation has many religious, social, and government programs that prevent something like that from happening.

The real question becomes: should one person have to die so that other people don't have to sacrifice Level 1 or Level 2 quality of life? If we answer, "Yes," then we are willing to sacrifice Levels 3 and 4 for the sake of Levels 1 and 2, which, as Mother Teresa said, is a terrible spiritual poverty.

But what about the argument

SHOULD ONE PERSON DIE SO THAT OTHERS DON'T HAVE TO MAKE SACRIFICES?

that abortion could be necessary to **prevent health problems for the mother**? It is irrational and unjust to put one person to death in order to prevent health problems for another person. Here, we are *not* talking about the life of the mother being in danger. Under some circumstances, it can be ethical to remove an unborn child from the mother's body if the pregnancy is causing an immediate threat to her life, even if doing so may indirectly result in the death of the child. The "life of the mother" issue is taken up in another part of the *Principles and Choices©* series. But when a pregnancy may harm the mother's health in a way that does not threaten her life, that is a different issue. It cannot be justified to knowingly cause the death of an unborn child in order to protect the health of the mother. The loss of life is disproportionate to the loss of health (the harm is incomparably more severe).

Another consideration is that, even if abortion were to prevent health problems for the mother and therefore preserve her Level 1 and Level 2 quality of life, by killing her own child she has lost the quality of life that could have been experienced in Levels 3 and 4. By loving someone other than herself and giving until it hurt, she could have experienced much greater purpose and meaning in life than by protecting her own health. Quality of life is most deeply felt when people are willing to give *until it hurts*. Jesus Christ gave of himself even when it required his suffering and death on a cross, so that we might have life.

© Leigh Schindler / iStockphoto

Why do people think differently when it comes to unborn children? Is it because we cannot see them, and so it is easier to abort them than to do the difficult work of figuring out how to love them? Is there another reason you can discern?

"Every child a wanted child."

This is a popular slogan in the abortion industry. At first hearing, it sounds like a good argument. **Shouldn't every child be loved and wanted?** Of course. But people who make this argument to support abortion are suggesting that children who are not loved and not wanted should be killed. This is not only illogical, it is cruel. And the finger is pointed at the wrong people.

If a baby in the womb is not loved or wanted, who has the defect—the baby or those who do not want him? Obviously, the problem is with those of us who have not learned how to love on Levels 3 and 4. Why should it be legal to kill children simply because the people who are supposed to be protecting them have become obsessed with Levels 1 and 2? When we hear a news story about a child who was harmed by a parent or guardian who did not love or want that child, our first instinct is

not to say, "Somebody should really end that child's life so that he doesn't have to be unwanted and unloved." Rather, our hearts break for that child, and we want to take him away and love him ourselves.

When people do not love their own child, a better solution would be to help them learn how to love, or to place that child with adoptive parents who can provide the love and care that every child deserves. Killing children is certainly not the solution to our inability to love. It is a symptom of our inability to love.

Furthermore, many children started out very unwanted by their parents; but then, after birth, their parents had a change of heart and found that they loved and wanted their children very much. Those who work at pregnancy resource centers (also called "crisis pregnancy centers") can recount many such stories, and there are numerous women (and men) who are willing to give testimonies of their

KILLING CHILDREN IS NOT THE SOLUTION TO OUR INABILITY TO LOVE

▶ Some people say, "This is my body, and if a baby interferes with my plans, I can have an abortion." Christ said, "This is my body, which will be given up for you." How are these two statements the same? How are they different? Which one is *agape*?

_____

change of heart. Use code **PCS1496** to be directed to some of these testimonies online.

Recall from Chapter 3 the difference between *agape* love, and the other types of love. Some people claim that abortion can be the most "loving" thing to do for a child. Margaret Sanger, the founder of Planned Parenthood, once said, "The most merciful thing that the large family does to one of its infant members is to kill it."[P] In other words, Sanger suggests that it can be loving to kill your newborn baby if your family is big. This is definitely not an *agape* view of love.

Agape love teaches that we should do everything possible to care for every child, even if it means sacrificing ourselves. That is not easy to do, but it is our most dignified purpose in life. This is why we were created. God did not make you for yourself. You were made to be a courageous hero to others. We were all made to give ourselves as gifts to others. God made us for *agape*, and when we love others in that way, we find deep happiness. Some of us will be called to do that in small ways. Others will be called to do it in very big ways. Do not be afraid of the ways that you will be called to sacrifice for other people—including your own future children. *Agape* is where

WE ALL HAVE A RESPONSIBILITY TO HELP PROTECT CHILDREN FROM ABUSE

we discover all of the things that truly make life worth living. *Agape* is where we encounter what is noble, good, honorable, and freeing.

A sub-argument of abortion supporters is that **there are some parents who are bad people, and they will abuse their children**. Certainly, we all have a responsibility to protect children from abuse, and society needs to work more diligently to prevent it, to identify people who are abusing children, and to rescue abused children as quickly as possible so that they can receive the love and care that they deserve. But killing children who might be abused if they are born is irrational and unjust. It does not solve the problem of child abuse. In fact, it is the worst kind of child abuse. Furthermore, it is impossible to predict in the womb which children will be abused and which ones will not be.

Ultimately, you will make the choice about the vision you have for yourself, for your future family, and for the kind of world in which you want to live. Will it be a vision in which we sacrifice others for fleeting pleasures and achievements? Or a vision where we face our challenges with self-sacrificial hearts and Level 3 and 4 attitudes? You have the power to make the right choice.

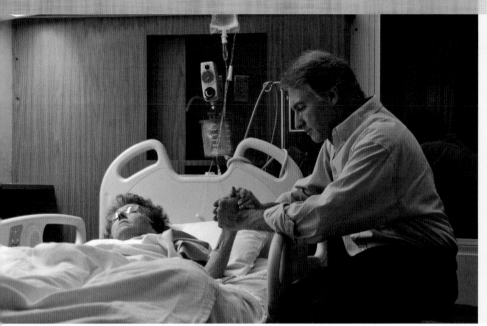

A LEGAL ISSUE OR A PERSONAL ONE?

Book 3 of this series explains why euthanasia and physician-assisted suicide should be *against the law*. This section lays out reasons for being *personally opposed* to euthanasia and assisted suicide.

EUTHANASIA

The word **euthanasia** (also known as "mercy killing") comes from the Greek *eu* which means "good" or "well," and *thanatos* which means "death." Literally, "euthanasia" means "a good death." In practice, however, the word means deliberately causing the death of a human being to end his or her suffering, such as a physician administering a lethal injection.

Physician-assisted suicide is defined as a physician helping someone to commit suicide, but not actually participating in the final deadly act. For example, a physician writes a prescription for a deadly dose of drugs, but the patient takes the drugs himself.

People who advocate for euthanasia or assisted suicide typically argue that it should be legal when people are terminally ill, very close to death, mentally competent, and choose it of their own free will. But others claim that restricting it to only the terminally ill and to the mentally competent is not enough. They want the law to allow physicians to put people to death who are elderly, disabled, or depressed even if they are not terminally ill. Some even want to make it legal to euthanize children and the mentally incompetent who cannot speak for themselves.

Only a small number of nations and a handful of U.S. states have legalized euthanasia or assisted suicide. In most places around the world, these acts are illegal for good reasons, which will be addressed in Book 3 of this series.

In this book, we will test these issues against the six Level 3 and 4 principles laid out at the beginning of this chapter. It should become apparent how many of the arguments against abortion evoke similar concerns about euthanasia and assisted suicide.

Before turning to the next page, it might be helpful to write out your own thoughts on the issues in the lined spaces to the right.

© Gilles Lougassi / Fotolia

GOING THROUGH THE LEVELS

The way people view happiness, success, quality of life, and love has a major impact on their attitudes toward euthanasia and assisted suicide. If people believe that the meaning of life is all about physical pleasure or ego-gratification (Levels 1 and 2), they will likely believe that they can no longer be successful when they are bedridden, weak, old, or terminally ill. They will think that life no longer has meaning or value, and will believe they cannot be happy in that stage of life. They may make statements such as, "I'd rather have someone end my life than be stuck in bed not able to do anything. The loving thing would be to put me out of my misery."

These attitudes are tragically narrow because they overlook the human capacity to find meaning through faith, hope, love, empathy, compassion, patience, generosity, forgiveness, friendship, goodness, and creativity. These profound Level 3 and 4 desires are often most poignant when people are weak, suffering, elderly, sick, disabled, or terminally ill. Legalizing euthanasia and assisted suicide only makes it easier for people to remain trapped in Level 1 and Level 2 beliefs about the meaning of happiness, success, and quality of life.

Often, people who favor euthanasia and assisted suicide claim that it should be used only in the most extreme cases, when someone is terminally ill and suffering becomes "intolerable and unbearable." By that, they mean a Level 1 or Level 2 interpretation of suffering such as having to give up activities one formerly enjoyed, suffering aches and pains, and losing physical independence and autonomy.

Physical independence means the ability to do things for yourself without relying on others for help.

When individuals view the meaning of their lives through Levels 1 and 2, they are often drawn into supporting euthanasia because it offers an escape when opportunities for physical pleasure and ego-gratification decline. Some people support euthanasia because they are afraid of pain (Level 1). Others fear that when they become ill or are close to death, they will lose independence, competitive advantage, or a sense of progress and accomplishment (Level 2).

In reality, modern medicine is so advanced that no one need suffer intolerable pain at the end of life, and modern technology offers numerous ways in which people can remain active, even when they are ill or disabled. You can learn more about this using code PCS1485.

Rather than helping people to commit suicide when they have lost Level 1 and Level 2 reasons for living, it would seem that a more compassionate response is to help people move to Levels 3 and 4, where the loss of physical health and autonomy doesn't have to be viewed as a loss of dignity and meaning. From a Level 3 and 4 perspective, there is more to life than enjoying past activities, being free of pain, and being autonomous. In fact, sometimes weakness and dependence on others are the very things we need in order to move to Levels 3 and 4.

People in Level 3 find quality of life in being with other people, caring for them, and doing good for others. Quality of life can come from helping family and friends get through tough times, listening to their stories or problems, inspiring others with wisdom, courage, hope, and love, or sharing faith or friendship. All of these higher level activities can be done from a hospital bed, a wheelchair, or a nursing home. Terminal illness does not reduce a person's ability to do these things. In fact, experiencing weakness or loss can actually make it much easier to do these things, since the person is no longer distracted by things that don't really matter, such as money, material possessions, achievements, and popularity.

When we are young, healthy, and independent, most of us try to enhance the Level 1 and Level 2 view of who we are. We try to look beautiful, powerful, independent, popular, and intelligent because we don't want people to think that we are weak. But when become old, disabled, or ill, and are facing the end of life, we *are* weak and everyone knows it. Keeping up the disguise and pretending to be powerful and independent becomes very difficult.

This stage of life can be the best time to let go of our disguises and learn how to love who we really are. Learning how to love our true selves helps us to learn how to truly love others. Love has a powerful way of coming alive the moment we stop focusing on material things and ego-gratification, and it can be stronger in the last few weeks of life than in all the years of perfect health that came before.

When people are dying, they are often able to let go of the anger or pain they may have felt against a friend or family member who hurt them. If we

SOMETIMES IT'S THE HARDSHIPS IN LIFE THAT LEAD US TO HIGHER LOVE, SUCCESS, AND HAPPINESS.

can inspire these people to choose love and hope instead of despair and suicide, the knowledge of their own approaching death may be exactly what they need to seek forgiveness and heal broken relationships.

People who have embraced Level 4 have all the benefits of Level 3, but much more. They find quality of life in listening to God communicating with them, knowing how much He desires and wants to be with them, and sharing their faith with others. Often it is much easier for people to share their faith with others when they are dying than at any other time, and this increases their sense of quality of life. Their lives really matter because they are making an ultimate difference to other people around them.

Even when we may be thinking that they are suffering all sorts of indignities, Level 4 people find their deepest dignity right in the midst of their terminal illness because they use their sufferings to bring God's love into the world. Furthermore, being weak and vulnerable increases ultimate quality of life because the more a Level 4 person is in need, the more she lets God in, and she is most in need when she is dying.

In short, Level 3 and Level 4 people have no use for euthanasia. Euthanasia and physician-assisted suicide would be the worst possible tragedy at a time when these people are able to do the most good with their lives.

LEVEL 3 AND LEVEL 4 PEOPLE HAVE NO USE FOR EUTHANASIA

EUTHANASIA AND THE LAW

At this point, some readers may be thinking, "What is wrong with allowing Level 3 and Level 4 people to enjoy the faith, hope, and love that they can experience during a terminal illness or disability, but allowing Level 1 and Level 2 people to choose assisted suicide?"

This would be the worst possible response—especially in law. When states legalize euthanasia and assisted suicide, it sends a clear message that, "When you are sick, weak, and dying, and you are stuck in Level 1 and 2 and have no hope or meaning left, we will not do anything to protect you and help you rise above this very limited and narrow view. We will just let you stay stuck in Level 1 and 2. We will agree with you that your life no longer has value and will help you to kill yourself."

This form of abandonment violates the very ground that gives government its legitimacy. A government does not have the moral authority to determine the quality of any of its citizen's lives. The government's responsibility is to protect all citizens equally, not to endorse a suffering person's view that her life no longer has any value.

Recall that the issue is not whether it should be legal for people to kill themselves. Legislation criminalizing suicide is arguably ineffective. The issue is whether the law should allow *other* people to decide that someone's life is no longer worth protecting and

Gabriel's Story

I have a son with Down Syndrome named Gabriel. My wife and I worked hard to mainstream him in the school system. Because he was older than all the other children, students at first made fun of him. But after a while, they began to see that he was really quite defenseless, that he did not have the aggressive instincts with which to respond to them, and that he needed them. Slowly but surely, they began to look out for Gabriel, and even to take care of him as a sibling.

The teacher wrote us a letter that Gabriel had been an invaluable contribution to the school, because he had single-handedly lowered the aggression level of the other students. She said: "Before he came, the children compared themselves to one another in a way that left room for only winners and losers (mostly losers). After his arrival, the care which they began to openly display toward him lessened their focus on themselves, and most of the children seemed to be happier. They actually enjoyed looking after Gabriel more than they enjoyed getting the upper hand!"

Gabriel was later pulled out of the school for medical treatments, at which point the aggression level in the school began to re-emerge.

© Gary Radler / iStockphoto

to *help* her commit suicide or actively *kill* her. To commit such an act is to make a judgment about the worth of someone *else's* life, which government does not have the authority to allow. The role of government is to protect life, liberty, and the pursuit of happiness—which means to protect the pursuit of all *four* levels of happiness, even for people who are stuck in Levels 1 and 2. A government has no authority to cut off the possibility that a person could achieve higher levels of meaning. But this is precisely what government does when it allows a physician to put someone to death. That is a value judgment that another person's life is not worth protecting.

Frequently, Level 1 and Level 2 people need our help to see the possibility of finding happiness and quality of life in Levels 3 and 4. When they do, it is usually not necessary to convince them that Levels 3 and 4 are better than 1 and 2. That truth is written into our hearts. But society should play the role of pointing towards the highest fulfillment that human beings can achieve—always pointing towards love, hope, compassion, faith, friendship, companionship, forgiveness, and the wisdom that comes when we listen to and learn from those who are weak, elderly, disabled, or terminally ill.

Advocates of legal euthanasia and assisted suicide tend to believe that people who are elderly, terminally ill,

Use code **PCS1483** to access vocabulary and other study tools for this chapter.

How do euthanasia and physician-assisted suicide add to our culture's obsession with a Level 1 or 2 view of **happiness**? How about a Level 1 or 2 view of **success**? **Quality of life**? **Love**?

© Scott Griessel / iStockphoto

or disabled have nothing left to give and nothing left to live for. While this may be true in Levels 1 and 2, they have so much to give and so much to live for on Levels 3 and 4.

It is especially important that we see this in people who are affected with Alzheimer's disease or other forms of dementia. They are frequently the first targets of euthanasia advocates, because they have such difficulty with the very things that communicate their ability to be involved in life—talking, remembering facts, recognizing people, and knowing where and who they are.

But when you spend enough time with a person who suffers from dementia and you keep a spirit of patience, compassion, and understanding, you soon learn that these people are very much able to relate to other people in significant and deep ways. They are able to remember significant moments in their lives. And if they were religious before the onset of their disease, they are able to relate to and love God in profound and meaningful ways.

CONCLUSION

Ultimately, human meaning and human dignity are not found in things, power, independence, popularity, or physical beauty. Instead, they are found in our ability to love and accept one another, and in our gift of self. Many leaders in our culture miss that point. They are willing to discard the very people we need to help us grow in love, compassion, and understanding. It is up to you to rescue the culture, to rescue the weak and dependent, and to rescue people from the Level 1 and Level 2 attitudes that lead to euthanasia and assisted suicide.

Persons who are weak and vulnerable are the keys to unlocking our own hearts. Even though they can sometimes be challenging, they draw compassion out of the rest of us. As we allow them to transform our hearts, they change us, and we discover a depth of love and compassion that would have been overlooked without them.

This appendix to Chapter 1, page 31 will outline a very simple form of one logical proof for the existence of God. Other more extensive proofs may be found online at www.magiscenter.org. Go to "Encyclopedias" under "Free/Resources," click on "God..." and scroll down to questions 4, 6, & 7.

A LOGICAL PROOF FOR THE EXISTENCE OF GOD

You may have learned in science that you cannot create something out of nothing. You cannot take nothing and produce matter or energy, or anything else. Nothing is nothing. There is nothing there. And nothing cannot produce anything. If you want to create something, you have to have something to start with, after which you can then produce other things.

You also cannot keep going back forever into the past, saying, "This thing caused that thing to exist, and that thing was caused by that other thing, and that other thing was caused by another thing, which was caused by another thing, which was caused by another thing..." and on and on. Why not? Because if everything was caused by something else infinitely into the past, then it would be impossible for enough time to pass to get to the point of creating you.

Think of it this way. Imagine that the universe is a great factory with a production line, and each part makes another part, which makes another part, until we get to you — the final product. If an infinite number of things were required to cause each others' existence before you could exist, then you would never exist. The production line would never get to you because it would take an infinite number of parts before you could be produced. Remember, an "infinity" means "unending" — it is always more than can ever be achieved. Therefore, the production line could never achieve an infinite number of parts, and would never get to you. You would not be here today.

To illustrate the point even further, imagine you meet a famous scientist and ask him, "What caused my existence?" The scientist might answer, "Your parents." And you might ask, "What caused my parents to exist?" To which the scientist would likely reply, "Your grandparents." Eventually you would have to ask, "Where did the very first human beings come from?" The scientist might answer, "From animals that evolved from lower life forms." And you would follow up with, "Well, where did the lower life forms come from?" The scientist would probably answer, "From cells that divided, and became more complex cells." Your next question, of course, would be, "Well, where did the cells come from?" And the scientist would respond, "From matter and energy." "But where did the matter and energy come from?" "From a big bang." "And where did the big bang come from?" You can see where this is going.

Everything that exists in the physical universe had to have something else that caused it to exist. Physical things don't just come out of nothing. But there had to be a very first Being that wasn't caused by anything else in

EVERYTHING THAT EXISTS IN THE PHYSICAL UNIVERSE HAD TO HAVE SOMETHING ELSE THAT CAUSED IT TO EXIST. GOD DOES NOT HAVE (OR NEED) A PHYSICAL BODY—HE ISN'T LIMITED BY THE PHYSICAL UNIVERSE. HE ALWAYS EXISTED, AND CAUSED EVERYTHING ELSE THAT EXISTS.

order to begin the process. That Being is called "the uncaused Cause," and started the whole process of causing things to exist.

An Uncaused Cause is a being that causes everything in reality to exist, but does not itself require a cause. It is eternal. It did not need to be brought into existence by something else.

Some scientists have argued against an uncaused Cause by proposing that aliens from another universe created our universe, sent physical matter here, and then caused a large explosion (the "big bang") in order to make energy and begin the process of creating life. You do not have to be a genius to figure out what the problem is: "Where did the aliens and their universe come from?"

Every time you answer that the very first thing was brought into existence by some other thing which itself needed to be caused by something else, you end up in trouble, because it wouldn't be the very first thing if it was caused by some other thing. And the very first thing could not have been created out of nothing, because that's impossible. Nothing can do nothing. Therefore, it cannot create. It isn't even an "it." Nothing is nothing.

Therefore, there has to be a Being at the very starting point of creation that was not caused by anything else, and so is eternal.

If you want a more technically precise way of looking at this proof, think about the following. Suppose that there is no uncaused Cause in all reality (inside or outside our universe). Then everything in all reality would be "caused causes." What does that mean? Let us use the letter "A" for an example. Since A is a caused cause, A is something that doesn't exist unless something else (let's say, "B") exists first in order to cause A. And then, once B causes A to exist, A can cause other things to exist. So we could say that A is nothing (zero) until B exists and causes it.

Now, let's return to our assumption, namely, that everything in all reality is a caused cause. Then everything in all reality is nothing (zero) until its cause exists and causes it. But since everything is nothing (zero) until its cause exists and causes it, then none of the causes exist. Which means that all reality is nothing! Even if you imagine that there are an infinite number of caused causes, they are still nothing (zero) because their causes cannot exist without existing causes. Remember, zero times one equals zero; zero times one billion is

still zero; and zero times one trillion is still zero. If everything is a zero until something real can cause them, then everything is zero (including you).

So how do we get out of this problem? There is only one way. You have to agree that there is at least one reality which is not "nothing (zero) until its cause exists and causes it." This reality must be able to exist without a cause, and so it is called "an uncaused Cause." If it is uncaused, then it is also eternal.

Proofs for the existence of God go on to show that this Being must be one (which means that there cannot be any others like it), it must be unrestricted (which means that it has no limitations at all), and it must be the creator of all else that is. We don't have the space to prove these steps here, but if you want to see these proofs, check out the website below.

Send your thoughts and questions to the Magis Center at **magiscenter.org**.

PROOF THAT GOD CAN FULFILL ALL OF OUR HIGHEST DESIRES

IS GOD ABSOLUTE TRUTH?

We saw in the section on "Crisis 3" that all human beings seem to desire absolute Truth. We want all the correct answers to every single question that could ever be asked about anything and everything. So we can also call this the desire for perfect Knowledge.

Many philosophers have noticed that since all human beings desire absolute Truth (all the right answers to all possible questions), we could not have fabricated the idea that absolute Truth exists. Think of it this way: When you are hungry, it is because your body is in some way aware that there is such a thing as nourishment to satisfy it. If there were no such thing as food, your body would not miss food and would not be hungry for it.

In the same way, when your mind is hungry for knowledge, it is because your mind is in some way aware that there is knowledge to be known. How does your mind know that? How do researchers know that there is knowledge out there that isn't known by anybody yet, allowing them to ask the right questions that are necessary to get the answer?

But even more than this, human beings don't just want some knowledge. We want all the knowledge that exists. We want perfect Knowledge. We don't want to be left in the dark or to be ignorant about anything. We would like perfect Truth so that we know what is really real and what is not. We want absolute Truth. So somehow, our minds are aware that absolute Truth exists,

and that awareness causes us to keep asking more and more questions.

You might argue, "Maybe there aren't any more answers, and all the answers that exist have already been discovered." But this can't be so, because millions of people around the world are still asking questions and getting more and more answers. What causes us to keep on asking more questions? How is it that we know that we have not reached everything that is to be known? How do we know, even when we have reached the highest known truths of mathematics, physics, and philosophy, that there is still more to be known?

The reason that this is such a problem for philosophers is that in order to ask a question, you have to recognize that there is a limit to the knowledge that we currently have, and every time you recognize a limit to our knowledge, you have to be already beyond the limit. Why?

Let us suppose that you are looking at a wall. You will not consider that wall to be a limit unless you have already imagined or anticipated that there is something beyond the wall. The wall is a limit to what is beyond it. However, if you do not recognize that there could be something beyond the wall, then you will just think of the wall as the end of space.

The same is true for limits to knowledge. If we had no sense that mathematics could go further than arithmetic, we would have stopped there and never come up with geometry, algebra, analytical geometry, and calculus.

How in the world can you be beyond every limit to knowledge so that you continue asking questions until you arrive at perfect Knowledge? It seems that you must have some kind of awareness of what perfect Knowledge (or

absolute Truth) might be, so that when you compare the knowledge you have right now to this "awareness of perfect Knowledge," you will always see the limits to your knowledge, and will therefore continue to ask questions until you get to perfect Knowledge.

This "awareness of perfect Knowledge" is not the same as possessing a clear knowledge of everything to be known. If we had a clear knowledge of everything to be known, we would not have to ask any more questions, because we would already know everything. So, our awareness of perfect Knowledge is something less than clearly knowing everything about everything. Our awareness of perfect Knowledge is just enough to get us to see limits to our knowledge, but it is not clear knowledge itself. So, what is it?

Many philosophers think that our awareness of perfect Knowledge is like a horizon—an awareness that there is something out in the distance beyond what we can already see. It is beyond us, and we know that something is out there, but we cannot perceive it clearly.

To understand what we mean by a horizon, you can think of Christopher Columbus. Columbus perceived a horizon out at sea. He was aware that there had to be something beyond that horizon, but he didn't clearly know what that something was. Since he was aware that there was something beyond the horizon, he perceived the limits of his Old World. He wanted to get beyond those limits, and so embarked for the New World. If Christopher Columbus had not been aware of the horizon, and had not been aware that something was beyond it, he would never have set sail. The idea of setting sail would not have even occurred to him. Why set sail if what you clearly see is all that there is?

It's the same thing with all of our questions. We are aware of a horizon, and we sense that there are answers which we do not yet know. If we did not have this horizon, then we would not recognize any limits to what we currently know. And if we did not recognize any limits, we would not ask any questions. And if we did not ask any questions, then we would make no advances in knowledge.

If you have followed this far, there is one consideration left. How did you get an awareness of a horizon of perfect Knowledge? You could not have learned about it from the world around you because if you look around you, there are no "horizons of perfect Knowledge" out in the physical world. There are trees, dogs, rocks, photons, electrons, and neutrons; but there are no "horizons of perfect Knowledge" that you can see with your eyes or with a microscope, or detect with any scientific instrument.

Perhaps you learned about it from someone else? That's not very likely because a horizon is precisely what you know to exist but cannot see clearly. Therefore, it cannot be described by anyone — not even the greatest genius. Try to describe to a person nearby what the horizon of perfect Knowledge is.

Then where did you get this horizon of perfect Knowledge? It would seem that the only source would be something that is or has perfect Knowledge, which would imply that such a Being exists. After all, if we possess a horizon of perfect Knowledge, then a Being which *has* perfect Knowledge would have to exist in order to present the horizon to us.

What Being would have perfect Knowledge? A Being which is perfect, and this would seem to be God. Thus, God would seem to have perfect Knowledge and could fulfill our desire for absolute Truth.

IS GOD UNCONDITIONAL LOVE?

Just as our desire for perfect Knowledge ("absolute Truth") must mean that human beings have an awareness of a reality that is or has perfect Knowledge, our desire for unconditional Love must point to the existence of a reality that is unconditional Love.

Test this thought: You want to be loved unconditionally. But has anyone ever been able to love you *unconditionally*? Really ponder that.

Most parents love their children — no matter what. But they don't always understand you, they aren't always there for you when you need them, and they sometimes put other interests ahead of you. Their love is conditioned by their limited human abilities. Your dog loves you. He doesn't care whether you clean your room or not. But your dog wouldn't love you anymore if you tortured him. His love is conditioned by how you treat him. Your friends love you. They like you just the way you are, and don't make any demands on you. But they sometimes say insensitive things, hurt your feelings, or can even lead you into doing things that aren't right. Their love is conditioned by the fact that they are imperfect too. Maybe you think that you have found the perfect person to love you who has never hurt you and who has always been there for you. But it is highly doubtful that this person will be able to keep it up for the long term. Even our own love for ourselves is conditioned. We sometimes don't love ourselves at all.

And yet, even though we don't seem to be able to get unconditional Love out of any other creature (including ourselves), we still desire it. Why is it that we grow so frustrated with our friends, our parents, and others, when they are not perfectly understanding or perfectly responsive to all of our needs? Why is it that we desire so much more than we have ever experienced? Our desire for love seems to go far beyond any worldly experience of love we have ever had.

How is that possible? How can we know what unconditional Love is in order to want it if we have never known or experienced it from any other creature? How do we even know what *perfect* Love would be like, in order to know *imperfect* love when we see it?

Many philosophers reason that the only way we can do this is because unconditional Love really exists, and makes its presence known to us in some mysterious way. We have an awareness of unconditional Love, and it draws us towards itself. It makes us want it, and when we try to get it from imperfect sources (like people and dogs), we become dissatisfied and frustrated.

These philosophers argue that this "unconditional Love" is God. If God is unlimited in His powers, then He would have to be loving. And if He were loving, then His love would have to be unconditional. If we say that God is *not* unconditional Love, then we would be saying that God's love is limited and imperfect like ours, which would, in turn, imply that God is limited in His power. But if we hold that God is unlimited in power, then it would seem that He would be unlimited in love. If God were unlimited in love, then He would be the source of our desire for unconditional Love. And if He were the source of our desire for unconditional Love, He could fulfill this desire.

IS GOD PERFECT JUSTICE?

As we saw in the section on Crisis 3,

we also desire perfect Justice, but we never seem to attain it in this world. In every conflict, there will always be someone who feels that his interests were not perfectly protected. No matter how diligent human beings are in trying to make things fair, someone is always going to complain about receiving less than what was deserved. This frustrates and disappoints us.

The same logic for truth and love applies here. If perfect Justice did not really exist, then we would not hunger for it. But we seem to have an awareness of perfect Justice and what it should be like, even though we did not learn this from the world or other people (who are not perfectly fair). How could we do that if perfect Justice did not exist? It must exist in order for all people everywhere to have a sense of it. Even little children who haven't been taught about it yet seem to know it — and they seem to know when they aren't getting it.

Many philosophers argue that this "perfect Justice" that entices us to want it has to be God. If God is unlimited, He would be perfectly Just, He would be the source of our desire for perfect Justice, and He could fulfill this desire within us.

IS GOD PERFECT BEAUTY?

Again, you can use the same logic here. When you look at a beautiful painting, or a magnificent sculpture or building, or listen to a great piece of music, or take in the majestic beauty of nature, you will always sense some imperfection or incompleteness in it. The painting is nice, but I don't like the color he used there, and I wonder what the woman looked like in real life. The sculpture is magnificent, but after I stare at it too long, it becomes a little cold, and hard, and…lifeless. The music is wonderful, but after listening to it too many times, it gets boring. The natural sunset over the mountains with the waterfall is majestic, but I wonder what's on the other side.

Our minds seem to have an awareness of perfect Beauty, and every time we see or hear something that is beautiful, we compare it to our awareness of what perfect Beauty should be like.

Recall our discussion about the harmony of form. When you have a beautiful musical harmony, you have notes, and the notes form chords, and the melody of chords all put together make you feel a kind of bliss. The complexity of the melody with the chords builds even greater, and you are in awe. Now, try adding this unity of forms in music to a grand architectural structure. You are listening to a beautiful Brahms symphony being played by the finest orchestra in the world, inside the dome of St. Stephen's Cathedral in Vienna. You are listening to the music and marveling at the grand arches and great pillars inside the dome. The visual harmony of the vast floor, the marble statues, the great carvings and gold accents united to the harmony of the music is even more beautiful. It is the middle of spring, and the flowers are in bloom, the birds are singing, and the sun is shining outside. All of these distinct forms coming together in a harmonized unity puts you into ecstasy.

Yet, even in this sublime experience of beauty, imperfections can be found. Eventually, this ecstasy will become boring as we long for something even greater — something more beautiful. How can we do this?

Many philosophers have argued that in order for us to be able to find flaws in virtually every form of beauty, we must have an awareness of perfect Beauty. When we compare our perceptions of worldly beauty to our awareness of perfect Beauty, we become immediately aware of the imperfections in worldly beauty, and we desire even more.

In order to have an awareness of perfect Beauty, it must actually exist. And since God is perfect and unlimited, He would have to be this perfect Beauty.

IS GOD PERFECT UNITY?

Human beings have a sense of what it would be like to be perfectly at home, to live in perfect unity, and to be at perfect peace with ourselves and with one another. You can prove that we have a sense of perfect home, unity, and peace, because we know when we are *not* perfectly at home, or in unity, or at peace. You could only know when you are *not* at home if you had a sense of what perfect Home was. But this world always seems to leave us feeling a little uneasy, a little unwelcome, a little out of place and alienated. So how could we know that we are not perfectly at home if we have never experienced perfect home? How could we know that we are not all living in perfect unity or peace if we have never experienced perfect unity or perfect peace?

Many philosophers make a reasonable argument that this is proof that "perfect Unity, Home, and Peace" really does exist and is present to your consciousness. They also argue that if God exists, since He would have to be perfect and unlimited, He would also have to be perfect Unity, perfect Home, and perfect Peace.

Notes

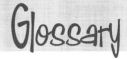

absolute Truth: All the correct answers to every single question that could ever be asked about anything and everything. Also called "perfect Knowledge."

***agape*:** (Greek, pronounced uh-GA-pay) selfless love that recognizes the unique preciousness of each and every other human being.

autonomy: The ability to do things for yourself, without relying on others to help you.

being with: To be with others in empathy, focusing on others instead of ourselves.

commitment: A spiritual, emotional, or intellectual bond with another person or course of action. A dedication, pledge, or promise.

common cause: To allow other people to share a common goal, rather than trying to do everything ourselves and get all the recognition for it.

contempt: To look at other people as if their lives are less significant than ours.

desire: An anticipation of something we do not yet have, which causes an emptiness inside and a yearning to be fulfilled. Every desire seeks fulfillment.

dignity: Being worthy of respect. All persons are worthy of basic human respect because they are made in God's image.

doing for: To do good for others. Doing something that benefits someone else.

dominant: Most important, or highest priority.

draw: (noun) Neither winning nor losing. Somewhere in the middle.

ego: Latin word for "I." Refers to our self; especially our self-esteem or self-identity.

ego-gratification: Finding fulfillment through being successful, powerful, popular, or better than others.

empathy: To feel what someone else is feeling; to identify with or understand the situation of another person by "walking a mile in his shoes."

***eros*:** (Greek, pronounced EAR-oss) Romantic love characterized by deep intimacy and commitment.

euthanasia — To deliberately cause the death of a human being with the intention of ending his or her suffering, such as a physician administering a lethal injection.

exclusive: Does not include anyone else.

external: Outside of ourselves.

Golden Rule: Do unto others as you would have them do unto you.

gratification: Satisfaction or fulfillment.

happiness: The fulfillment of a desire.

higher levels of happiness: Experienced through the heart, intangible. They require more personal sacrifice, last longer, and are deeply fulfilling.

humility: A virtue in which you don't think of yourself as greater or lesser than you really are. An honest view of yourself compared to others.

immediate gratification: To receive physical pleasure right away, without having to wait.

induced abortion: Intentionally causing the death of an embryo or fetus by a direct or indirect action.

intangible: Something that cannot be perceived through the five senses. Instead, it could be perceived through the heart — like love.

intimacy: To open up the deepest parts of yourself to another person: physically, spiritually, emotionally, and psychologically.

intrinsic dignity: The true worth and goodness inside of every human being, including ourselves.

intrinsically valuable: To be valued for who you are as a human being, and not for anything you have or can do.

Glossary

justice: Goodness or rightness; giving someone his due, or giving someone what she is owed.

love: To desire the good for someone else so much that it becomes easier to do good for that other person than it is to do good for yourself.

low self-esteem: A sense that we are no more valuable than things.

lower levels of happiness: Tangible, require less personal sacrifice, don't last very long, and are not deeply fulfilling.

materialism: Finding fulfillment through material possessions and physical things.

miscarriage: See *spontaneous abortion*.

momentum: Once something gets going, it keeps going by itself.

perfect Unity: Feeling as if we belong in the universe, are at home in the cosmos, and are at peace with everything that exists. Also called "Perfect Home."

perfect Beauty: Beauty in its purest, most perfect form.

philia: (Greek word, pronounced FEE-lee-uh) Friendship; the kind of love that involves give and take.

physician-assisted suicide: When a physician helps someone to commit suicide, but does not actually participate in the final deadly act. Such as when a physician writes a prescription for a deadly dose of drugs, but the patient self-administers the drugs.

principle: A basic truth or law that applies universally and helps shape our attitudes and beliefs.

pro-life: The position that all human beings, including the unborn, elderly, terminally ill, and disabled, are sacred and should be protected by law.

purpose: The aim or goal toward which someone is striving. The reason for which something is done or created. We will view our purpose in life according to the desire that we give priority.

quality of life: The way we judge the worth, happiness, or success of our lives.

seven deadly sins: Sins that lead to other sins and vices. Also called the seven "capital" sins. They include pride, greed, lust, envy, gluttony, anger, and sloth.

social issues: Concerns that affect many members of society. They are usually controversial and deal with questions of right and wrong.

spontaneous abortion: (See also *miscarriage*.) When the embryo or fetus dies unintentionally because there is something wrong with the pregnancy or because something traumatic happens such as a fall or a car accident.

storge: (Greek, pronounced STORE-gay.) Spontaneous feeling of affection or delight toward someone or something.

success: Achieving a goal.

tangible: Can be perceived through the five senses.

terminal illness: An illness that cannot be cured and will result in death.

transcendent: Beyond physical. Something that is really real, but we cannot see, taste, touch, hear, or smell it. Examples would be love, truth, or justice.

uncaused Cause: A being that causes everything in reality to exist, but does not itself require a cause. It is eternal. It did not need to be brought into existence by something else.

unconditional: Complete or guaranteed, with no conditions, limitations, or strings attached.

A Alfie Kohn. "In Pursuit of Affluence, at a High Price." *New York Times,* February 2, 1999; www.alfiekohn.org/managing/ipoa.htm

B Catharine Pratt. "Five Tips for When You Feel Like an Outsider or Like You Don't Belong: What to do when you feel like you just don't fit in." www.life-with-confidence.com/feel-like-an-outsider.html

C Steve Kelly, "Ike's story is about much more than one touchdown run." *Seattle Times*, October 10, 2010. seattletimes.nwsource.com/html/stevekelley/2013128361_kelley11.html

D Lawrence B. Finer, Lori F. Frohwirth, Lindsay A. Dauphinee, Suscheela Singh and Ann M. Moore. "Reasons U.S. Women Have Abortions: Quantitative and Qualitative Perspectives." *Perspectives on Sexual and Reproductive Health*, 2005, 37(3):110–118.

E VM Rue et. al., "Induced abortion and traumatic stress: A preliminary comparison of American and Russian women," *Medical Science Monitor* 10(10): SR5-16, 2004.

F M. Gissler et. al., "Injury deaths, suicides and homicides associated with pregnancy, Finland 1987-2000," *European Journal of Public Health* 15(5):459-63, 2005.

G VM Rue et. al., "Induced abortion and traumatic stress: A preliminary comparison of American and Russian women," *Medical Science Monitor* 10(10): SR5-16, 2004.

H JR Cougle, DC Reardon & PK Coleman, "Depression Associated With Abortion and Childbirth: A Long-Term Analysis of the NLSY Cohort," *Medical Science Monitor* 9(4): CR105-112 (2003). See also DC Reardon, JR Cougle, "Depression and Unintended Pregnancy in the National Longitudinal Survey of Youth: A Cohort Study," *British Medical Journal* 324:151-2, 2002.

I VM Rue et. al., "Induced abortion and traumatic stress: A preliminary comparison of American and Russian women," *Medical Science Monitor* 10(10): SR5-16, 2004.

J DM Fergusson, et. al., "Abortion in young women and subsequent mental health," *Journal of Child Psychology and Psychiatry* 47(1):16-24, 2006; DC Reardon, PG Ney, "Abortion and Subsequent Substance Abuse," *American Journal of Drug and Alcohol Abuse* 26(1):61-75, 2000; D.C. Reardon, P.K. Coleman, and J.R. Cougle, "Substance use associated with unintended pregnancy outcomes in the National Longitudinal Survey of Youth," *American Journal of Drug and Alcohol Abuse* 26(1):369-383, 2004; PK Coleman et. al., "A History of Induced Abortion in Relation to Substance Abuse During Subsequent Pregnancies Carried to Term," *American Journal of Obstetrics and Gynecology* 1673-8, Dec. 2002; and PK Coleman, DC Reardon, JR Cougle, "Substance use among pregnant women in the context of previous reproductive loss and desire for current pregnancy," *British Journal of Health Psychology* 10, 255-268, 2005.

K PK Coleman et. al., "State-Funded Abortions Versus Deliveries: A Comparison of Outpatient Mental Health Claims Over Four Years," *American Journal of Orthopsychiatry* 72(1):141-152, 2002; and DC Reardon et. al., "Psychiatric Admissions of Low-Income Women Following Abortions and Childbirth," *Canadian Medical Association Journal* 168(10), 2003.

L P.K. Coleman, V.M. Rue, C.T. Coyle, "Induced abortion and intimate relationship quality in the Chicago Health and Social Life Survey," *Public Health* (2009), doi:10,1016/j.puhe.2009.01.005; and PK Coleman et. al., "Predictors and Correlates of Abortion in the Fragile Families and Well-Being Study: Paternal Behavior, Substance Abuse and Partner Violence," *International Journal of Mental Health and Addiction*, DOI 10.1007/s11469-008-9188-7, 2008.

M N. Maconochie, P. Doyle, S. Prior, R. Simmons, "Risk factors for first trimester miscarriage—results from a UK-population-based case– control study," *BJOG: An International Journal of Obstetrics & Gynaecology*, Dec 2006. Abstract available at www.blackwell-synergy.com.

N VM Rue et. al., "Induced abortion and traumatic stress: A preliminary comparison of American and Russian women," *Medical Science Monitor* 10(10): SR5-16, 2004.

O DC Reardon et. al., "Deaths Associated With Pregnancy Outcome: A Record Linkage Study of Low Income Women," *Southern Medical Journal* 95(8):834-41, Aug. 2002.

P Sanger, Margaret. *Woman and the New Race*. 1920. (New York: Truth Publishing Company).

Index

Index